Harmless Medicine

Harmless Medicine

Justin Chin

Manic D Press
San Francisco

Some of these poems first appeared in slightly different versions in the following magazines, webzines, and anthologies: *Isibongo, Frigate, Web Del Sol, Comet, Hogtown Creek Review, 6,500, Sundog, Sway, Queer Dog* (Cleis), *Shampoo, Kestrel, Traffic Report, Walrus, The Gay & Lesbian Review, The World In Us* (St. Martin's), *The Outlaw Bible of American Poetry* (Thunder's Mouth), *Take Out* (Asian American Writer's Workshop).

Cover design: Scott Idleman/Blink

Library of Congress Cataloging-in-Publication Data

Chin, Justin, 1969-
    Harmless medicine / Justin Chin.
        p. cm.
    ISBN 0-916397-72-6
    1. Asian American gays--Poetry. 2. Asian American men--Poetry. 3. HIV-positive men--Poetry. 4. Asian Americans--Poetry. 5. Gay men--Poetry. I. Title.
    PS3553.H48973 H37 2001
    811'.54--dc21
                                                    2001004181

In memoriam

Jhan Dean Egg
Rick Jacobson
David Grossman
Wayne Corbitt

Contents

I.

And at the ninth hour, Jesus cried with a loud voice, saying, 'Eloi Eloi, lama sabachtani?' which is interpreted, 'My God, my God, why hast thou forsaken me?'

— *The Gospel According St. Mark. 15:34*
(King James version)

Undetectable

The space pod shrunk to microscopic
proportions with its inhabitants aboard,
injected in the vein of the terminally
ill coma patient. Traveling in the
bloodstream, we peek into the human body:
tissue, cell, organ, blood, lymph.
Every lucid hue taken away
by the black and white television set.
The mission: to reach the tumor,
to blast it with the specially designed
and shrunk laser gun. There are
complications of course, (why should
fiction not have a smudge of horrible reality?),
and Raquel, plucky scientist in her daring
skintight curve-enhancing wetsuit, swims
in blood to do something heroic,
but she is attacked by white blood cells, (eek!),
envisioned by the special effects department
as crunchy foam fingers, not unlike
the white fungus delicacy of soups
in Chinatown restaurants; deed
done, more white cells attacking,
oh how will they escape? Through the eye!

Cure or Blight. Who is
the foreign body here?

There is a battle in my body. Every day
a small chunk of me is given up in this
microscopic war. Small flecks of cells,
shreds of tissue, muscle, skin, bone
disintegrate, turn to junk, float
through my body and are pissed out.

This atom, this molecule, this bond
between them will quell the virus.
Squash it into almost nothingness,
into something so small, smaller
than it already is, so it won't show,
cannot be counted,

like ghosts and gases, its true existence
undiscovered, lurking
ready to kiss or kill. Undetectable.

Only in B-movies:
foreign body kills foreign body,
chemicals and petri dishes don't lie,
easy redemption, happy ending.

Everyday, a small bit
of myself dies
in that chemical battle.
    An undetectable bit
of myself dies everyday.

I get tired easily. I take more naps.
I dream less.
I smell like the medicine chest.
Some days I think I can
feel every single cell in me.
I can feel every single one
that dies.

Apocryphal Medicine

Cumulonimbus clouds float at foot level.

A Chinese man in a bowler hat walks by.

Plastic bamboo, the size of a brittle child's forearm, painted with a motif of caterpillars on its stems.

A nation mourns the death of a supermodel, flawless girl with perfect skin and handbag husband.

Fried Camembert cheese topped with cranberry sauce is served for breakfast.

A digital clock on a street in Paris flashes the temperature, $0°, 1°, -1°, 1°, 0°, 1°, 0°$, mad Morse, a demented binary code.

The souls of the immortals dwell with exotic birds in the cosmic mountains, believed to be the place between heaven and earth.

A boy blows on embers to light the hearth, a man with an old monkey perched on his shoulder watches from a dark corner.

Asparagus, grown like veal in a small wooden box so it remains thin, tender, sweet.

The kitchen god's mouth is smeared with honey so he will only report the sweetest news.

A sketch of a dead child set in a gold frame, hung in the hallway.

A lipstick print on his hip, herpes scarlet on his flesh, white as a milk bubble.

Poppies decorate the war memorial, a monument to the failure of politicians.

A Magritte painting dipped in barbecue sauce.

Surrealist Bookmark

Directions for use:
1. Find the line in the book where you have stopped reading. Place bookmark elsewhere in the book.
2. Place bookmark in a stranger's book.
3. Go to a hospital and leave bookmark in a patient's book. You may also leave bookmark at a public pay phone in the facility.
4. Place bookmark in a book that has yet to be written.

Warning:
May cause reader to lose place in book. Extreme disorientation may occur. Loss of connective thoughts and lucid speech akin to dementia may set in. Do not operate pasta makers. Do not mix with herbal remedies. May cause liver damage, kidney stones, cerebral hemorrhage and ulcers. May cause extreme euphoria. May cause false increase in self-esteem. Peripheral nerve damage occurred in 21 percent of test subjects who used a placebo bookmark. Some users report hallucinations of Parisian cafes. Visions of God, Buddha, Vishnu, Jacqueline Susann and Donald Duck may occur in a small percentage of users. Cheese, curry and spring rolls may never taste the same for some users.

If any of these reactions occur, discontinue use. Remove bookmark and place it in a moist, calm, dark, quiet place until side effects subside.

Poison

Four men carry one,
each holding a limb,
wife trailing crying:
bit by a scorpion;

the evil culprit,
black in a jam jar,
rattles against glass.

Poison in the blood,
no feeling in arms and legs.

On the surgical table,
my father strategically
inserts seven fine
needles, newly acquired
acupuncture skills from Taiwan.

Soon, the man walks shakily,
slight limp out of the clinic.

Maybe there was more,
I'm sure there was more
to it than that,
but an eight-year-old boy
in pajamas and slippers
killing time
in his parents' workplace,

discovers that

> (and it marks him
> for the rest of his life)

there is a cure
for poison in the blood

put there by scorpions,
snakes, spiders, centipedes
and demons.

And for a while,
the fatal, cancerous
world that spins
towards hell and destruction
slows its revolution,

and there is more
        day and more night.

Faith

Lisa gives me a bracelet,
    a Buddhist trinket she got
when her family went to temple,
a custom to see the beginning
                of each year.

A delicate thing,
        beautiful in its symmetry:
Eighteen beads the unruffled color
of a Chihuahua puppy's tanned fur,
two transparent beads on each side,
    seven more tanned beads each,
and in the center, a large white bead
holding a convex corneal
                slip of plastic,
a white eyeball that reveals,
when you hold it up to light,
the Buddha and his slippers.

If my mother ever saw me wearing this,
she would be gravely upset, grieved;
this small trinket troubling
her firm Christian beliefs,
those she inculcated in her sons.

I do not practice Buddhism.
A charm has only as much power
                as one puts into it.
I wear it because it is such a pretty thing.
And the person who gave it to me
cared enough for my protection:

a reason greater than any faith.

Once, in a Chinese restaurant,
I saw a group of school kids kick
the shrine sitting beside the fridge:
the pot of joss sticks, the tea cups
tumbled over, and the oranges scattered

across the floor, the fat laughing Buddha
fell face down, as if doubled over in hysterics.
The perpetrators of this horror were angered
by the shop proprietor's refusal to serve them.
But did they not realize what they had done?
    Were they not afraid?
Was not the proprietor's faith in his god's
powers to take retribution
       greater than the boys' faith
that the god they had kicked was powerless?

I'm told tales where Buddhist shrines,
Hindu temples, voodoo floats, Christian crosses
    were desecrated
and the persons responsible came
to mysterious and disastrous ends.

Can faith equal faith?

    Is there any equivalence,
or are we weighing elephants against toenails?
What exists in our world that would allow
us to measure such inequivalence,
      to balance the scales of
culture, faith and fear?

Many months ago, I believed
that my room was haunted. I felt a presence
sitting on my bed, and the cat was sleeping
in her sweet purr on the porch.
          I tried to wake
but felt held down by an invisible force,
my head pressed against the pillow,
my voice taken away from me: I could not
even call out to wake myself up.
    All I could do was pray in my mind,
and pray I did. I suddenly awoke
in a dark still room. This is how I knew
I still believed in the God of my youth.

    Can faith equal faith?

Do gods of one faith take care
        of the believers of other faiths?
Who will protect my god
when he falters
        and his faith fails?
Do the gods of one faith take care
        of the gods of other faiths?
Can it change the spleen of our lives?
Of what we've seen and done,
and what has been done to us?

        Look to Job —
family decimated, crushed
        under eight tons of party lights,
lost, scabbed, ill and tempted;
patient, unquestioning and faithful.

        Idiot simple,
it sometimes seems.

Never mind earthquakes, floods,
storms, collapsed buildings,
serial killers, car accidents,
famine, endless war, another car bombing,
pestilence, flesh-eating bacteria,
untold hatred, the unforgivable,
forgetfulness, revisionism.

Here is my blood-stained faith.
On my wrist, in these boxes of pills,
in this blood test, tubes of scarlet proof,
in this inoculation, dead cells
of ancient diseases flow with the fur pelt
of the dog that bit and bit right
through to bone and brain; it is
in this string of obituaries, this book
I am yet to read, this newspaper, these words,
this cure, these half-truths that burst into full
truths, these lies that rot into complacency,
the memory of all the dead and all the living
behind and in front of me; this
is my blood-stained faith.

I Buy Sea Monkeys

In the pages of DC comics,
The New Teen Titans save the world

from the world, and stays evil
forces in their dark places;

a page tucked in between their noble
tasks: the promise of bringing life

to life. The drawing shows a family.
American 1950s compact and nuclear:

Crayola flesh-colored parents and children.
The females have eyelashes, ribboned bows, pearls.

The males have bow ties; Dad has a pipe.
Sea monkeys. What miracle of science

could fathom this? Monkeys who live
in the briny depths, who learn to

do acrobatic tricks, and set up house.
How I yearned for a box of miracles,

my own laboratory to bring life
to these amazing pets. My parents

were too sensible for such comic book
chicanery. And the local toy store

would not honor the coupons.
I was too young to understand

the concept of a money order.
I was sea monkeyless

for twenty years. Adulthood
confers certain privileges.

Mr. Frankenstein with charge card.
I finally got my kit.

Crystals dissolved in pure water,
the small plastic tank set

to the right pH to bring life,
eggs poured into the primeval

quench, and in the dissolving
swirl of egg and liquid and fuzz,

little swimming things
swim and paddle against the current.

Not like monkeys in the zoo or even
in the trees. Not flesh-colored.

No snazzy Abercrombie & Fitch tie,
nor Benetton sweaters. How

at the Seattle Aquarium, a small child,
at that wondering age I was

when I wanted those aquatic monkeys,
asks his mother, what are the sea horses

eating? They look like sea monkeys,
she says, and his kiddie eyes that scanned

some other comic book too intently
as I did, start to tear up.

Dream Pet = Fish Food.
Magic sputters into another gutter.

We grow up and figure out the truth,
we realize how hard it is

to maintain and take care
of life, even the ones

that deceive you, especially
the ones we cherish:

I get lazy, preoccupied, go on trips,
holidays, blank days, and return,

the tank is deep-sea green,
saturated, oxygen starved,

little tatters shed and floating
like flakes of a million dead things

in the ocean. In the convex magnifying
bubble of the tank (so you can see the life

you brought), all is exoskeletons,
all is dead, all minute souls given up.

All but one little monkey,
swimming with all his might, all

his filaments paddling in the murky green,
shimmering like the last good cell

in the last good body.
He will live another six weeks,

longer than all his family and species,
then he too will shed his skin one last time,

wonder where everyone has gone
and go there too.

Final

When I die, I want to be cremated
and buried in the Cimetiére des Chiens
on the outskirts of Paris.
    On my grave, I want a statue
of a dog, viciously digging into the mound,
and pulling a stone hand out with its mouth.
    A plump cat will be balanced
like a Bulgarian acrobat on the dog's back.
    On the cat's head, a mouse —
though a hamster or chinchilla is acceptable too —
will be holding onto the cat's ears
as if it were riding the rodeo for the fifth year.
The rodent will have a top hat and tails on.
Resting on the top hat, a butterfly.
    And on the tip of the butterfly's left
wing, two ladybugs
                dancing the foxtrot.

The inscription on the tombstone will read:

> *Despair not, no strange fate befalls.*
> *On fearful night in heart, no heroes raised.*
> *No monsters vexed, no affliction reached.*
> *In dreams of outlaws' tears, this blessed rest.*

Contents Page to the Book of Poems I Have Yet to Write

Chinky Nightmare #1: Giant Non-Poisonous Snake
The Moo Shu Chronicles
Cities That Die At Easter
Quality Shopping at Warehouse Prices
Eat My Chewy Fuck
Escapade
Do You Believe In Life After Love
Papercuts in the Afterlife
The Connoisseur of All That Matters
Explosions of Randy
Radiation Flinch
Beginnance
What Violence Tears Apart
The Silence of The Earthworms
Chinky Nightmare #2: Killer Ceiling Fan
Use Ticks
Health Declaration of Petrol
I Want Japanese Animé Hair
Penguin Lazarus: A Resurrection
I Did Not Know Shame Then
Oops...I Did It Again
Ow...Don't Do That To Me
Ew...Go Wash Your Hands
Argh...What Are You Doing With That
Poison and Calamity
Pork Is My Friend
Lucifer's Lock of Pubic Hair
Stamp Collecting In The Third World
Gerald Has A Nosebleed
Lungfish Trauma
The Glue Cannot Hold
What Life Will Separate
All The Crack Whores Have Passed Out From Heat Stroke
Mung Bean Fever
Extreme Solitaire
Gary's Making Soup
The World Is Not The Place To Eat Cheese

The National Museum of Health and Science

Skeletons of children, aged one month
to five years in ten growth intervals;
the small bones and rickety shells hung
on tinny hooks, none of them will annoy
on planes anymore; what could such small
children know of death, that they should be
stripped of skin and flesh, muscles boiled off
from their little chubby frames and displayed;
no more rope games and ball games,
no more childish giggles and pranks, instead

of endless playgrounds, they're hung
in this musty case for all of history,
a lesson, a page of a biology
textbook come to deathly life.
Jars of aborted fetuses,
pickled in an unnatural vinegar.
Cross-sections of men and women's
throats, those who have died by choking:
the trachea stretched back to show the choking
hazard: piece of beefy gristle, dentures;

the tongue pointing upward to taste the air
above the formaldehyde, razzing the air
denied them. The tattoo of a flapper girl
falling backwards, caught by a billowing
confederate flag, her white skin
of legs and a promise of a good time
on sun-wrinkled cancered skin, removed
from a 62-year-old sailor two years ago
to study his hideous crusty melanomas.
Somewhere there's an old sailor with no

skin. A hairball extracted
from the stomach of a twelve-year-old
trichotillomaniac, the clump of hair
in the perfect shape of her stomach
since it was cut out in 1954. Has she
seen the source of her pain

since then? To perform these exacting incisions,
an array of knives, lancers and scalpels,
laid out on cold reflective surgical trays,
slicing ready, dormant.

Microscopes, ancient: glass lenses
held in place by metal cylinders;
and modern: electron machines
that bombard frozen less-than-razor-thin
slices of tissue, so that it explodes
in a supernova of discovery,
revealing its secret world of lattices,
matrixes, how the cells cling
together to make up the lumbering
lummox peering into the case.

The Medieval practiced art of bloodletting
leaves us its artifacts of suction cups,
lances, beautiful blades, tin pans
to catch the drippings; glass stained with
the rust of some old old blood. Who
did this iron-russet stain heal? This punctured
cure based on an idea that the body was a being of
black bile, yellow bile, phlegm and blood,
and their perfect harmonious balance.
Monthly, and quarterly drawings

sucked out into stoppered test tubes,
carefully color-coded vials, catheter-
fine porcupined proboscis, mosquito-
jabbed into the junkie-fat vein
in the crook of the arm; the hurt
never equals the cure. In the National Museum
of Health and Science, press this button,
hear the click, softer than a new toaster
going to work and you will see what is
causing our endless unsetting mourning:

tiny tornado that rips through,
pulling great things set for decades out by
their roots, cracking foundations; here

it is, captured on a slide, so colorful,
a kaleidoscope, a test for colorblindness,
not a virus so small it sneaks right through,
leaving its scar tracks, claw marks,
muddy slug–like footprints, across
our weakening bodies and our fine
fine hearts. Push this next button: now see

how a healthy human blood cell, long forgotten
by bodies grown familiar to shopworn, corrupted
cells, is attacked by the virus; the internal
battle, seen only by the highest powered
microscope, an absent blind careless god,
and the scheming devil; see how the cell, happy
carefree, once invincible, crafted
in God's image, meets the evil
seductive wily virus; Eve in the Garden
of Eden with the serpent, Adam

is watching, preparing the sauce for
the forbidden fruit dessert; see
the virus sneaking into the healthy cell,
see how they meet, see how they dance,
see how it crushes like a bad relationship
on an afternoon talk show. See, here
is the real virus, the placard says, push
this button and another million colors
light up the screen, another kaleidoscope,
— is all disease so vibrant and luminous?

Is this what this is, the deadly
brilliance of our national shame,
the lay of our global suffering,
the crux of grief and disgrace, the stuff
of failed heroes and unlikely villains,
cures that fail faster than fate, hope
and quackery, medicine and faith,
a generation stained by rage, smudged
by resignation, the evidence of our
splintered unspeakable sadness,

the accumulation of what remains.
In the still, processed air of the hall,
the engine of the display hums, and in
the National Museum of Health and Science,
all the species, dead and alive, abortions,
tissue slices, stuffed things, pickled
livers, preserved organs, and premature
deaths, long mourned no more, all grind
to a slowest stop to witness what we have come to.

Mirage

The stuff of cartoons,
B.C or Fred Bassett jumps
into the swimming hole of clear rippling
water only to have it be

hot sand, concrete;

mirage.

Fetched back from another day of
the kindergarten sandbox, my head
wedged between the front seats
of the family Morris-Minor,
the air-conditioner blasting
in my face; Mom points it out,
and there it was, twinkling,
like Christmas promises,
in the noontime distance:

rain slicks on the Kuantan asphalt.
We speed into the puddle,

but there's no gleeful splash,
just the dust of the tropics.

Older, I learned
how mirages are created.
In my ruled school exercise book,
I drew fluffy clouds, an unforgiving sun
with radiating zig-zags blazing
its melanoma-causing rays,
and little arrows
representing how rays of light travel, how
they refract through the ruled
lines of air, imaginary
layers of heat and humidity
until they hit a point on the ground
where they reflect back into
a big eye hovering over

the whole scheme.

A mirage is nothing but
a reflection of
the sky above.

The water that will save you
when you are abandoned in the Sahara
is only the endless sky. Might
as well wish for Coca-Cola, Fanta Grape,
Vietnamese iced tea.

Look above to the heavens:
See the majesty of what may not be there.
How the clouds hide what's behind their formations.
How optical illusions create UFOs
        and monstrous prehistoric birds.
The most brilliant stars have already burnt out.
The giant gaseous planets, ringed
        with seven moons and four ice rings
are a mere period in the night sky, seen
only twelve nights a year.
                Connect the dots
of constellations, and see
the worse stick figures, nothing at all
like lions, warriors, ice cream scoops,
grizzly bears or fierce gods.

For those stranded in the desert,
some mirages can be more elaborate,
brutally realistic. The laws
of physics and science, of light
and its rays are unflinching, unmerciful.
The oasis and palm trees,
the succulent dates and two-humped camels,
are reflections of the real
thing far far away, but channeled
through heat and sky,
and projected onto desperate retinas.

A mirage is something
        like hope,
but not it.

Magnified

My brother got a microscope for his twelfth birthday,
hope of the family, excelling in all subjects, graced
with straight A's and a brain for chess, the gift
was an early enticement into the illustrious world
of medicine; but he was too busy playing football
to bother with it, so after it lay in its box
for months, I took it on as my own. Dinky, plastic
thing it was, but I felt like a scientist in a foreign
TV movie. I set the instrument up in our study room,
used the table lamp and shone its harsh bulb onto the reflective
mirror, redirecting the light through
the slide and into the magnifying eyepiece. The microscope
set came with ready-made slides: a tiny piece
of pink feather, a sliver of an unnamed insect's wing.
But I wanted to see what I wanted to see. I learned
how to prepare slides. I took a sewing needle
to the spore bags underneath fern fronds and scrapped
spores onto slides. (I saw round black saucers.)
I stripped leaves and petals of their epidermis
by painting them with Cutex nail varnish and carefully
peeling that layer of hardened goop off. (I saw
brick walls of cells in perfect order to respire and
to photosynthesize.) I looked at onion skins. (I saw
exquisite paperthins.) I looked at droplets of swamp water.
(But I saw nothing.) I caught ants — the small black ones
and the ferocious Kerringa fire ants — and pinned them
under glass slides. Still alive, their segmented bodies
struggling, magnified to horror movie proportions.
The red ants snapped their pincers in despair and anger,
the black ones waved their six legs in tired resignation.
Once I turned the magnification too high and the lens
crunched into the slide, cracking the cover slip, squishing
the ant. Its grizzly death, full of juice and torn
segmented bits, magnified 200x. I looked at moths' wings
and butterflies' wings, mosquitoes' proboscises, beetles'
legs. I looked at hair, saliva, dead skin peeled off from a sunburn, dried
blood from scabs, toenails, a drop of blood.

Later, my dad let me use his microscope. An impressive
thing: heavy and metal, not the light plastic toy I had
been playing with. And the magnifications were much higher.
This was how adults saw things. And everything I had seen
magnified before, was remagnified into a grander scale.
Cells broke into smaller cells, colors broke into a myriad
of more color and detail, light into more light. Amazements
into marvels, marvels into epics. The droplets of swamp
water that revealed nothing before now teamed with wriggling
things and strange life. The drop of blood now took on
more red, and life's movement shivered within that smear
on the slide. I looked at my semen and saw sperm cells,
the little bits of me wiggling their tails, swishing away
to a futile ruin. Everything I had dared to cram under
the lens and everything I could scrape and mount onto glass
slides was made up of small things of such delicacy,
and smaller things even, that when assembled
together constructed a greater beauty. The dead bits
lying on those slides were to face up to the harsh
realities of the world's atmosphere, to give flight,
to fight, to hunt, to repair, to prettify, to live as much
as the fragments, the living crumbs, held together.
And everything that was examined and dead, peeled
off and amputated, separated from its larger life,
was renewed with as much, even more
glory than the day, and the day after that, imagined.

Lesson 1.0

Between patients at the dispensary,
and ever one for an educational opportunity,
Mom shows me how a pill dissolves
in the gut after it is swallowed:

In one soupspoon of water, a capsule;
In another, a chalky pill.

Soon, the blue and orange plastic
    that's not plastic, it's gelatin
turns soft and collapses,
spilling its contents, white powder
dissolving into the spoon of water.
    The pill turns to paste,
and helped with a stir from
the little finger, dissolves too.
Ready to be sucked in
by the stomach, ready to do
its work of healing and fortifying.

Both: sorely bitter to the taste.
So savage on the tongue
that they must be repackaged
into neutral forms,
pretty colors.

"Why don't they make it sweet,
put sugar in it?"

The answer is simple, obvious:
"Some medicines just cannot be made sweet,
  otherwise they will not work."

Nipa, Encephalitis
(Malaysia, 1999)

Spread by mosquitoes who bite swine then bite humans, spitting the horrible virus from bloodstream to bloodstream, gushing across amusement park channels of blood vessels to brains where it tents up and wrecks. These are the first symptoms: the loss of motor functions, limbs turn to quiver, loss of consciousness; then horrible death. The infected pigs in their corrals are easy to spot. They squeal as if the butcher had just killed their litter, their back limbs collapsed underneath their fatty pink bodies. Soon the shivering takes over their entire bacony bodies and they bleed from their mouths and anuses. Occasionally, some bleed from their snouts or ears. Rarely, but it happens, a sow will bleed from her dangling nipples.

The epidemic had been spreading among the pig farms on the West Coast for months. Pig farmers have been dying, sent to the hospital, dying. An epidemic easy to contain, the battle plan already written into the annals of medicine for decades, but in this nation of lunar cycles and gold mosques, nothing is that easy. *God's will*, the authorities said. *Pigs are unclean, it is Allah's will.* And so pigs die, pig farmers die, and the plague hangs and hovers as gossip and fear. Mosquito spray is sold by the carton and more toxic insecticides are pumped into the air of more houses.

The market price of pork suddenly becomes unbelievably cheap. Neighboring nations police their borders against the bloody infected meat. Businesses, restaurants, grocers, and butchers slump into ruin. Oh what will John Loo, Pig's Organ Soup King, do? What will become of his 14 hawker stalls? Where will the pork-fat Chinese businessmen get their nourishment to close that next abalone deal, score those fourteen crates of Mandarin oranges before Chinese New Year? How will the Mandarin Hotel manage dim sum Sunday for the congregation of the United Methodist Church after-service luncheon? The people start to panic and the government has no choice.

The authorities send in the army to gun down the pigs. Specially suited workers haul the carcasses away in their med-evac vans. Thousands of pigs, infected or not, shot to prevent the spread of this dread. Nature has a way of having its way: the virus snakes its way across species; an act not seen before, and the crowds gasps in amazement. Dogs, cats, cows are also contracting the virus, all bit by those pesky mosquitoes. There is no pork, at least very little pork on the market. And it is now unbelievably expensive, for the daring who dare chance it, or those who know how exactly the virus is spread: blood to blood. Cooking well will kill that microscopic terror. Cooking with garlic and spices will make it tasty. But it is also the time of the great onion shortage. Supermarkets, grocery stores, roadside vegetable stands are out, down to a few measly shriveled bulbs.

Onions are now shockingly expensive too, as if it were rare fruit. Something about civil wars in India, something about the floods washing away all those fragrant succulent bulbs. That layered staple in kitchens from farmers' mud huts to movie-star condominiums. The government has fallen in India because of onions. Riots have broken out in border towns of India and the military has been called in to restore order. The mood, carried across border checkpoints and state lines, rippling through unfragrant kitchens, is tense; there are relatives, recent immigrants, ties, obligations, duties, unforeseen burdens, all resting on those tear-inducing bulbs.

It's now BYOO. Mom packs onions in her handbag and brings them to the hawker center so we can have some with our satay dinner. Mom's handbag: Paracetamol, Dramamine, Ponstan, Immodium, Gingko, bee pollen, Nivea Vitamin E cream, Estee Lauder lipstick, mother-of-pearl lined lipstick mirror, coin bag with secret pocket for cash, hairbrush, onions. She suspects the satay man has kept half her onions. She wants my dad to go over to the stall and get the rest of them back, either it goes on the plate, into her family, or back into the handbag.

Now it's in the evening newspapers: pig farmers are trying to smuggle what's left of their pigs out of the country on small motorized boats. The coast guard is called out to patrol the waters and to intercept suspicious powered sampans that may be hiding a parcel of seasick hogs. The Malay government and army killing the Chinese pig farmers' livelihood starts tremors of racial tensions; the withered grapevine rustles with rumors of race riots, yet again. Mad rush to supermarkets, to stock up on canned sardines and luncheon meat, instant noodles and corned beef, in case a curfew is called. Local police fan out to hardware stores to order the proprietors not to sell knives and cleavers to anyone for a fortnight.

After months of plague and error, the health authorities trace the source of the virus: giant bats that live in the dense rainforest. Bats who came out of their lush habitat as agriculture moved into theirs, to eat the crop of fruit farms and bite a few animals along the way. News bulletins flash, TV programs are interrupted, the announcement is made: the pig extermination campaign is a success. The epidemic is stemmed, the dying stops, new pigs are bought, businesses straggle back onto the marketplace, and here we are, back to onions and pork and dinner.

(Animal) Species I Have Eaten

Chicken, of course, and its liver, kidneys, gizzard, and intestines. I have also eaten its scaly feet but I do not care for them. Duck and its liver, and especially its crispy roasted skin. Goose and its liver. Quail. Sparrow (curried). Iguana (tastes like snake). Snake (specifically, python, tastes like squab). Pigeon (tastes like chicken). Kangaroo (tastes like duck). Alligator (tastes like pork). Horse (so I'm told). Dog (as meatballs). Rabbit (as stew, and as barbecue). Venison (as steak and as burger). Frog (legs and breasts). Turtle (in soup). Cow (call it beef, if you will, in all its blooded forms, and especially its stomach and intestinal lining). Lamb. Veal. Pig (call it pork if you want, and its stomach, intestinal lining, sexual organs, and lungs). Ox (tail). Goat (call it mutton if you must, some people object to its strong distinctive smell). Then there are the fish species: Haddock. Bream. Cod. Red Snapper. Grouper. Monkfish and its liver. Catfish. Stingray. Yellowtail. Salmon (and its cholesterol-high eggs). Tuna. Crab. Prawn. Crayfish. Lobster. Shark. Cuttlefish. Eel. Octopus. Squid.

There are also variations of unknown meats in sausages, Spam, deviled meats, corned beef, cold cuts, pizza toppings, ballpark hot dogs and roadside vendor wieners.

And then, there are eggs. The accounting of which has not yet been undertaken.

Grave

In the harsh glare of an easily
reprehensible life. The channel changer is lost
in the crack of an infinite sofa.
        Everything falls apart, everything breaks
down, torn into a million
                fragments, Jericho everyday.

I want to be the blameless
victim in this canceled puppet show,
the marionette every mother loves, the one
souvenirs are modeled from.

                (In that lifetime, Elton John will write mushy ballads just
                for me. Michael Jackson will want to be my best friend. He'd
                take me to Neverland Ranch, and by the llama feeding trough,
                he's say something like, "You're a great guy, don't give up,
                stay positive!" And I'd say, "Michael, you fucking idiot, I *am*
                positive." And he'd say, "Oh, you're so funny! Would you like
                to touch Bubbles?"
                And I would.)

In the crux of my hollow innocent youth,
I believed that my teddy bears had feelings.
        To cure me of this, my guardians made me give
them to the church missionaries' children.
Scrubbed-clean rosy-cheeked blonde kids who smelled
of sweat and talc, who were in constant
wide-blue-eyed bewilderment as to why
they were profusely perspiring in the tropics,
instead of living out some winter wonderland Bobsey Twins
fantasy, who were oblivious
to their parents' desperate efforts
to save the dusky masses, ignorant enough
to believe in the secret lives of stuffed animals.
        I could not eat animal crackers
because I did not want to hurt the poor things;
but, braised the right way, I could eat
any part of a pig, starting with the head,
working on the soft flesh around the eyes,

savoring its raspy tongue with a dipping
sauce of ginger, chilies and lime.

Oh blameless innocent victim.
What measures a lifetime?

I used to have this theory about how
much life a human body could hold.
It all had to do with the number
of heartbeats. Each human assigned a number
determined by an unknown power cascading
over the dark waters of the unformed Earth.

For some, it was a magnificently high number,
seen only in Richie Rich comics, and for others,
it was frightfully low, like twenty-six.
No bargaining, no coupons,
no White Flower Day sale, no specials. Once
you hit your number, you croak.
          I imagined the angels in heaven
and the demons in hell gathering to watch
the counters turn, like how I enjoyed watching
the speedometer line up to a row of similar
numbers, and especially when the row of
nines turned into
                    the row of zeros.

Oh blameless innocent victim.
What measures eternity?

An eternal damnation. An everlasting love.

I could not imagine the night sky
stretched out forever, so I decided that it came
to an end at some point, by a velvet rope it ended
and beyond that rope were row after row of cushioned seats,
          a majestic cosmic theater,
playing every movie I can remember.

I want to be able to evoke
those blameless and innocent days, to revel

in their ignorance and goodness
as if they have the power
    to protect and to heal,
and to strengthen,
and to bring me to safety
    long after all other resources
        were exhausted.

But I emerge anew in the wreckage,
blinking in the sunlight,

the residue of salt water in my belly.

You know what they say,
God never closes a door before making sure
that the windows are barricaded
and the fire escape is inaccessible.

I used to know how to stop the revolution of planets.

I used to know how to save the world.

Now, I don't know anything anymore.

Harmless Medicine

The odds:

Chinese satellite spins out
of orbit and reenters the earth
atmosphere where it breaks
into twelve equal pieces; ten
chunks plunge into the Salton Sea
in a mad fizz; one piece, the tail,
hits a tin shack in a palm oil plantation
in Kelantan; the twelfth piece hits
you on the back of your head as you carry
a box of newly bloomed white narcissus bulbs.

———

At one time, they told me that the voices
in my head were the devil; at another time,
China; and another, the medications.

———

The water that pools at my feet in the shower:
amber, ochre against the white tub.

There are days when I think
it might be the chemicals leaching
out of my body;

or is it the soot of the city, the dust
and particles from the construction
behind my apartment, they're building
new expensive modern lofts,
I've left the windows open again;

or am I just dirty?

but this somber color:
as if I were washing orchid roots in the bath.

The leper rings his bell.

The leper bangs his gong.

The leper begs for alms.

The leper salves his sores with Tiger Balm.

The leper straps on a Stratocaster
    and tries to play a mean solo,
but his fingers snap off at the knuckles,
    like a jigsaw puzzle coming apart.

Ha Ha Ha Ha | Ha. Ho Ho Ho | Ho Ho.   Hee | Hee Hee
Hee Hee. | Doo   Doo   Doo Doo | Doo. Tra La La | La   La. ||

---

catheter:

blood flows in endless freeways
of arteries and vessels, exerts

a pressure, a force that drags

spiders into my veins.

Watching Manet's paint dry.

Alternatives:

The Gingko's not working.
The St. John's Wort I'm advised to avoid.

The Milk Thistle is for something else.
The Selenium makes me bloat.
The Ma Huang gives me palpitations.
The Multivitamins are good, but watch the Iron content.
The Echinachea does something weird.

The
  Gingko is.   Not.

Work.   Ing.

―――――

"...*left this life, caught his last, left the stage, left us suddenly, passed away, communes with the spirits, passed away peacefully, died peacefully, made his journey home, suffers no longer, succumbed, passed peacefully from this life into God's hands, soul left his body for his last eternal voyage, departed, left us...*"

―――――

Insomnia intermezzo:
2:01 a.m.: documentary of ants mating
3:36 a.m.: machine that slices, dices, and makes life so easy
4:54 a.m.: looks like joan crawford in the twilight zone
5:15 a.m.: strange dream of canoeing in the sewer
7:32 a.m.: plane crash off the coast of southern california
8:01 a.m.: endless chatter, time for work

―――――

What is the taste of a tear
and how is it indistinguishable
from the taste of a thousand seas
of tears: a body of water so vast
and so salty, new life begins in it

everyday; and strange marine mammals
not seen even in the deepest plunge
of the earth's oceans live and thrive there.

―――――

The Proper Dosage:
2 tablets 3 times a day with a full glass of water.
1 capsule 2 times a day after a full meal.
2 tablets 8 hours apart on an empty stomach.
3 capsules 4 times a day with fruit juice.

The Problem:
If I leave San Francisco on a airplane at 9 a.m. traveling eastward en
route to Kuala Lumpur, and the plane crashes into the Himalayan
mountains, and I crawl out of the burning wreckage and find myself in
the mythical land of Shangri-La, where no one ever gets sick and no
one ever dies, calculate how many pills I should save from the flaming
cabin luggage, when I should take them, and what I should do about the
refills.

If at the same time, my evil doppelganger, the one responsible for feral
cat attacks on pharmacists, leaves Singapore at 8 a.m. and travels
westward, but with stopovers in Hong Kong, Karachi, Dubai, Abu
Dhabi, Copenhagen (cheap flight), and arrives at New York La Guardia
in the middle of a snowstorm, determine what I should do about the
pain in my spine, and the adverse reactions to the prescribed antibiotics.

(please show your working calculations)

Bonus Point Question:
Calculate how many pills it takes to fill the Royal Albert Hall.

————

There's a trick I'm teaching my body to do,
to not mind the aches, the flu-like symptoms,
the slow brakes and creaking joints,
to ignore the nausea and the deathly fatigue.

I'm teaching my liver to love these toxins.
I'm teaching my heart to pump in regular 2/2.
I'm teaching my lungs to be swollen and greedy.
I'm teaching my stomach to do my belly good.

I'm teaching my blood to not mind the chaos.

Suture:

flesh to catgut kissed;

camouflage: scars,
indelicate pigmentation;

disguised as healing.

———

What wrecks us. What takes us
by the scruff and throws
us into the breakers, drags

us along the reef, drives
splinters into what's
left of our bodies.

What allows us to stand
this chaos in our veins.

———

Ignore the sky and all that is in it.
    Do not look at the ground

or where your feet are planted.
    What can it matter?

Trust where your body falls,
    the air it takes in,

the sweat of strangers,
    the ground it sleeps under.

———

Day starts as night.

And the evening and morning
were the next day.

II.

where there were no spiders I saw spiders
penetration till it comes like the flood

— Patti Smith, *Witt*

O Sweet Cookie

You have the character and determin1ation to realize hopes and will marry soon.

knife edge
dangle precarious

Discover your companion's world. Two worlds are richer than one.

heart

One is your lucky number.

lie in state

between knife and heart

Your lover will never leave you.

blood(y) space

Trust him, but still keep your eyes open.

cut   remain   in blood

You are next in line for promotion in your firm.

space between words
mere purpose   no fate

The eyes believe themselves, the ears believe other people.

deliver

blood(ed)
start with

knife

Good health will be yours for a long time.

: cut heart   endure

It's an excellent day for dusting. Start with a few old dreams.

: fuck heart   exists

You should not return to the past to revive an old relationship.

: divide heart   permanence

You will do well to expand your business.

: perform surgery on heart   salvage

You are careful and systematic in your business arrangements.

: bleed poison from heart   liberate

You will make many changes before settling satisfactorily.

ends   always ends
on heart

Pride Pissed

The weak ones.
Left for the poor at heart.
Regret.

Delight. Now.
Night comes early.

A fantastic story.
An exquisite mirror, given in love.

Beauty is the least of it.
Each lover prepares us.

A plague that steals souls.
A plague that steals language out of the faithfuls' mouths.

A game where you try to toss pennies into the gaping mouths of
ceramic frogs.

All actions. Nothing more. Hopefully.
Weeds probably.
Weeds.

Worse.
Our descendants will know.
They will be prepared.
A big ball. A messy tango. Too many to count.

Even today.

The show goes on.
But no one sees.

These are my lover's eyelids. Torn off like rose petals, melting
in my hands like ice unpacked in sawdust.

If only.

That's the way we know. Were taught.

Worth an alchemist's secrets.

Nothing.

A stolen language unto its own.

A wave crashing against the rocks.

Memory. Amnesia.
With nothing. Yet remembering everything.

The tendency is to conceal.
A natural part of our civilization is the beautification of
unpleasant truths.

We do as we must.

We are taught to stand still.
To expect the best in life.

In a great world, one would never ever have to consider the
consequences.

Hopeless romantics to think such thoughts.
Like a junkie dipping into his granny's purse to steal milk money.

Give the spinster a hand, a good pat of the back.

A state of emergency.

Not the exception but the rule.
A protest. A sea of people marching and chanting, carrying signs with
bewildering cryptograms.
Ribbons are tied to anger and passion on the streets today.
Passion is linked to patience and pity.

Obvious. A good beat.
Mere plaything to impress. To maintain appearances.

Murder. Plot.
Abandoned to a pack of wild alligators.
Merely disfigured.

Look. Look.

The new mirror.
Flowers are growing.
Such an impossibility in such a place.

Only crab grass.

All that incessant gray soot. Depressing.

A bad plague.
Only a soothsayer can save the show now.

If only.

These are my childhood scars.
I have counted every single one of them.
In my mind, they are worth a princess's dowry.

A spectacle. An audience.

Fit in or be damned.

Noise. A closed window.

Alleviate these stories.
Demand plot, narration and fantastic things to believe in.

Reading and re-reading. To lose.

Bright lights.
On stage: Freak or Actor. Model or Sack of Dung.

The heretics meet under a fiery moon to say goodbye to another
thousand years.

Machinery. Cruel industry.

All hope lost.

Noise. Window. Poison. Ivy.

Midnight.

Addicted. Affections.

Jealousy. Possession.

Plague. Acquired.

Passion. The suffering.

Assigned pain.

The Mother holds the bleeding body of the newly crucified.
It becomes real.

Sheer enterprise.

How do you say goodbye to a monster that harbors so much ill
will, so many sad deaths.

                                                    Killing fields.
We look for the gaps, the glimmers in between.
Hope for.
                          Uncommon courage. Good times. Celebrations.

This beast.

                              Or a fire.

Prepare for the worst.
                              Hopeless.
Same.
One should be warned.

I carry my belly. I bear the burden. The deformity. The protruding head.
The bellybutton.
                                        There is no warning ever.

No one ever locks language up.
In the open. Thieves come.

See.
                        A pretty mirror.
                        Cracked.

Meat cutter.

She owned a horse farm.
With a volcano in the middle of it.

                              How beautiful. How queer.

                    True.
We should be flowers.
We needn't wait to be asked.

Admire the one who steals language like a thief in the night.

I turn mute. Then Speech.
Then mute again.

My beautiful corpse that I carry in my belly.

Scrumptious splendid debt.

In memory.
                    In all aspects of life.
The domain over which the lie reigns.

After the ball.
A plague. So graceful. A dance.
          This is the scar. The rotting corpse.

                    The very first time.

What will have changed in a thousand lifetimes?
What indeed.
                                        Luck alone.
                    Time. Time.

A thousand years stacked upon a thousand, and yet a thousand more
on top of that.

This is the scar. In memoriam.
The finishing touch.

All down the food chain. All consume this lost blood.
                              It is worth an exquisite valor.

We lie or not.

We lie like mad.

We. Witness.

Wound of a thousand fires.

I carry a war in my belly.

Last Worry

1.

This is nothing.
    Been worse.

Turn around   gone around
          & gone.

    Count to three (no one comes).

2.
                     /break/

Slap.   The pluck.
Hiss.
      Background chatter.
Air-conditioner hum.
           "what will it be"
Violet rumble.   (slide/slide).
Wired. Comes   & goes.

               /in the break/

3.
Sucked in   held,
blown out   gone.

    Linger.

4.
The rose is sticking in my back.
The thorns poke just beside the spine.

Some little prick.

Poem for Somebody

Two cowboys dancing
    heads tilted
the brims of their hats
    fit in planar angles:

Two ringed planets
    in a mescaline discotheque
defying Newton's Laws
    twirling physics

in revolution
    around the mirrored ball.

Wound

I.
A man who worked
on her father's chicken farm

held his hands out to her
showing where the machinery

had severed his fingers.

Come feel the skin, dear
see how it feels.

II.
Pieces of my lover's fingers
lie in a muddy field in Vietnam.

Phalanges   Landmines
Used condoms   Padi

III.
A great notebook
sheet upon sheet of grained paper

stained with huge blots of blood
asymmetrical Rorschach test

Chinese calligraphy
of an unknown language.

Neo Testament

Jesus had a twin named Ted. Ted Christ. Ted was neither godly nor evil. He was just indifferent. Jesus hated Ted. He prayed everyday for Ted's crib death, and God listened. Jesus soon regretted his decision and held his breath until God resurrected Ted, but on a different day, so he would not have to share birthdays.

As a baby, Jesus loved to tongue all the other babies in the village. The virgin would constantly find him at the neighbors' house or at the daycare center with his fat holy tongue stuck onto some bawling infant's face. She was grossed out and embarrassed but what could she do? After all, he was the son of God, and she was afraid of losing her maternity and health benefits. So she let him alone, the holy terror. Benjamin Spock and a whole legion of child psychologists yet to be born would not have approved. But then again, what could anyone do or say, without the little brat having a temper tantrum and bringing plague on the town?

Instead, the virgin spent most of her day perfecting her macramé skills. She made amazingly complicated potted plant hangers which her husband Joseph the Carpenter sold for a nice price at the flea market. She was not concerned with the commerce of her art, it was the work that settled her, for she knew that each knot and twist of raffia and rope was a portrait of the tangled knotty web of despondency and sorrow that clung to her heart. She was melodramatic in that way, even long before ladies' romance novels were invented.

Jesus and Ted did not get along. Jesus always felt that Ted got special treatment, and he complained bitterly about it all the time, even though it was he who was treated with exceptional indulgences. It got especially ugly when Joseph the Carpenter made a ukulele for Ted so that they could have musical accompaniment as they sang the Carpenters' Greatest Hits together while tending the sheep.

Jesus hated that rustic life which smelled of dung and sawdust; he preferred computer hacking and going to raves where he grooved like he was the son of God. Jesus was a great breakdancer, capable of the most complicated spins and pops and breaks. He dreamed of forming his own breakdancing posse, and he tried to enlist Ted, who was not only uninterested but also terribly uncoordinated. Each rehearsal proved to be increasingly frustrating, and Jesus popped a wave and threw his hands up in despair. Breakdancing was far too much of a cross to bear, but it was one that he was fated to bear by himself.

The virgin tried to read to Jesus, but he preferred to sit in his beanbag with a plate of cheesy nachos watching all the mini-series, documentaries, animated cartoons, and films about his birth and life and death and resurrection.

The Virgin read the resurrected Ted assorted magical realist novels, Beat poetry, and the good bits out of *Vanity Fair* when he was a day old. Soon he was performing miracles, even as a mere toddler. While the other children were crawling into cupboards underneath the sink to eat bleach and stuff rat poison up their tender butts, Ted was turning water into wine, wine into Diet Coke, Diet Coke into Diet Pepsi, Diet Pepsi into an assortment of high-energy low-calorie isotonic sports drinks. He started walking on water and waterbeds, making the blind see, healing syphilitic cows, making lame sparrows fly and shit again, healing botched boob-jobs among the temple sluts. He taught his mother how to appear on sides of buildings, in tortillas, bearclaws and other breakfast pastries. He learned how to multiply fishes and loaves of bread, create new concoctions of spring rolls, and he invented nouvelle cuisine.

Jesus hated Ted's ambition, but he took good notes of Ted's achievements and knew that one day he could plagiarize them to great effect.

When he was 18, Ted left home to become a bohemian poet, but his beatnik stylings proved to be too far ahead of his time and he was stoned to death.

Jesus was happy. Now it was his turn to shine.

Beefy Fag

We are so beefy and we are so gay,
we work on our pecs at least 8 times a day.
We're Tigre & Bunny & Butchie & Gee
cruising in our Geo Tracker, we all go "whee"
to the tunes on the Savage Garden CD.

Posing at Starbucks, we bitch about the twinks.
In our dungarees, we look like truckers, you think?

Here comes Tigre, so furry and so butch.
And here's Bunny, showing off his cooch.
Butchie woofs at Bunny, Bunny woofs at Gee
Tigre woofs at Butchie, Butchie woofs at he & he & he.

"Who Let The Dogs Out?" Bunny he will say.
And Butchie and Tigre will giggle and act all gay.

Oriental Suture

I. SKIN HATED:

Peeled off like the crispy delectable skin of roast duck, delicious sunburn.

A reflection broken by sweat; by a greasy kitchen painted nausea pink.

Tongue wrapped around your lover's face, lips puckered, ready to receive dark hollow kisses.

Butterfly plunges the knife into her belly, crumples onto the stage, kimono billowing, revealing her cellulite-encrusted chubby white legs and big European-shaped buttocks.

II. CRUSHED:

The actress wears her curlers like a crown of thorns.

A reflection broken by the clanging of an alarm clock.

Every move rains brimstone on your angelic face, pierces straight through your forehead; your palms blister, your head cracks with raw vascular seizures, your eyes turn bloodshot, your throat strangles.

The black cat dances feline around her prey before baring her pearly claws and yellow incisors to the rip of flesh to lip smack.

This is not the war we enlisted for.

After the honeymoon, food tastes like metal brushes, smells like roses.

III. CHINAMAN'S DECAY:

Corpse shrouded in jade, stealing brilliance from every spotlight on the stage; blink, and wild limbs fall away.

A strobe of flesh hiding a conquered fortress surrounded by jungle fires.

A tissue with a lipstick kiss print, fragile as an exotic butterfly near extinction, chloroformed and mounted on acid-free hardboard, framed and hung on the wall, saved for all who pay admission.

A black pearl you keep under your tongue.

III.

This is the voice of the sandstorm, the voice of the unplayed hearts.
These are the endless children rolled over and over at nightfall.

—William Dickey, *T.S. Eliot at One Hundred and Seven*

Imagining America

1.
If the world has seen America through the movies,
I imagine how the world has seen me.

If America has seen my homeland through the movies,
I imagine how America has seen me.

The has-been actress on the telly plumps pity with a side of
      Christian do-good. Her red fingernails rest on the knobby
      head of a belly-bloated child,
even as the promises of the spilled semen of green cards & Amex
      holidays slash their way across the Third World.
Even as the gay community clamors to join the military,
a drag queen in Malaysia bleeds to death after a group of soldiers
      hacks off his penis to teach him a lesson.

                                "Take it like a man, boy."

Even as GIs & soldiers go on R&R in the sunny Third World,
      screwing their way into the psyche of a queen named Exotica,
a 16-year-old boy dies because of the infection caused by the sex toy
      that shatters in his rectum, shoved there by his Big Daddy who cries
      & moves on to the next one.

                                  "Take it like a man, boy."

Even as AIDS inches further into wounds of the Third World,
the AIDS-infected flight attendant lives out the rest of his life
      in Bangkok, screwing without a condom & living out his dream
      of spreading his love to a bevy of beautiful boys.

                                  "Take it like a man, boy."

Go ahead & plumb the Third World for your sense of spirituality,
      your fuck-me-all Godhead fix, rest easy in your futon feeling that
      you're making an affirmative gesture.
If you can't afford the sex tour, join the Peace Corps.
Even as the Land of Opportunity devours its poor, tired, hungry masses
      yearning to breathe free, we're asked to be silent, quiet, don't make

waves, don't offend, do nothing, buy a new pair of sneakers, sit back
& enjoy your favorite decaffeinated red, white & blue cola.

I'll take it like a man.
I'll take every inch of it like the man you want me to be, like the man
    I'll never be, like the man the world wants me to be, the man
    Asian-America wants me to be, the man my dog wants me to be.
Take it like I got a chip on my shoulder, —hey, what's your chip?—

If America has seen me through my cuisine,
I imagine how I would taste.
On the days when I've been the hero, the monster,
the slut, the piece of shit. Some other permutation of myself.

If I have seen myself through the movies,
I imagine how I have seen myself.

I'm tired of explaining how it feels.

2.
Foreigner, stranger:

    The hidden face of our identity.

    A border between human bodies
    patrolled by suspect, guarded

    by hounds trained to sniff
    out every inch of your body.

        Swimming past Kansas.

Native   tourist   other.

Citizen:

The foreigner is detested
because we refuse to recognize

the foreigner within

ourselves.

3.
Bruised sky scarred
with tissue shreds of clouds
guide the flying night insects bug-speed
into the windshield of the car.

Each greeting of abdominal fluids
become bats with outstretched
inviting arms, trash
on the road becomes roadkill

good enough to eat,
and the marshy grasslands, steep cliffs
that shear steeply, a skid mark
away into dark nothingness.

The redwoods wrap around the bends,
clinging to sickly fog,
the decreasing speed limits,
until the cricket silence pulls

us into a meandering calm.
Should we have stopped
at that last truck stop,
or that last motel with the free

cable and heated swimming pool?
Should we have stopped even at all?

Another roadside diner, and another
Grand Slam breakfast that tastes

of the same cheese, the same grease,
as every other on this tarmac circus.

The familiarity, the lack of surprises,
the same security of regular
unsurprising coffee in regulation white mugs,
filled with hot coffee that cools fast.

Night breaks into chilly
bluish dawn, the rain darts
on the glass windows. The first
trains rumble by, headlong

into the day and noon and fog
and still of our ever-changing country.

4. (Fleet Week, San Francisco.)
These are not angels,
for what angels are driven by men,
        and what angels spew
such smoke and pomp and earthly noise.

    Seven fighter jets,
the glint of afternoon sun
on their navy tails and wings, fly
            in V-formation: metal ducks
heading south to bellicose warmth;
a show of warring plumage, fluffed for
        an infinite wintry aggression.

        And on the ground,

children cling to mothers' pants
        in awe and wonderment, a streetperson
waves, certain dogs yap in utter

confusion, tourists and locals
        look up at the swooshing spectacle.

And on the ground,
an old Asian women drops
her shopping basket, throws herself
to the ground in a fetal ball,

    her wrinkled old arms wrapped
around her head, covering ears
and thin hair, waiting

        for that moment of impact.

But there is no
    sharp churn of shrapnel and earth and fire
on the ground.

She picks herself up off the pavement, her eyes
ignore those of an old Asian couple
who dashed for cover in a nearby doorway;

she gathers her basket from between two parked cars,
brushes herself off and rushes to the market;
a new truck of fresh chickens has just unloaded.

    No bombs dropped here today.

    All shelled out.

    Strategically deployed many years ago.

    But only some have started to detonate.

These angels are blue indeed.

5.
American dogs cannot eat chicken or tomatoes or they will die. If your
dog dies, you can be arrested & put in jail.

There is vegetarian lard, meatless sausage, turkey pork, wheat-free bread,
non-dairy milk, & fat-free sugar.

Everyday, a new cereal, a new cola (diet & decaffeinated), a new chocolate bar, & a new shampoo are invented by scientists working in big factories.

For your health, there are vitamins from AA to ZZ, herbal extracts to supplement the vitamins, oxygen tablets to supplement the herbal extracts, bioenzyme capsules to supplement the oxygen tablets, powdered Chinese medicine to supplement the bioenzymes, yoga & pilates to help the Chinese medicine absorb properly, aerobics machines to help you get the most of the yoga & pilates, crystal healing to help center you after the aerobics, aromatherapy to take the edge off the crystals, & psychotherapy for all-round general health & well-being.

The ultimate plateau for any celebrity in America is to become a spokesperson for anorexia nervosa & bulimia. Celebrities also lend their winning personalities & star power to educating the public about a whole range of health concerns, social & political issues & making sure that American history & America's place in world history is not forgotten.

A tragedy is not considered tragic unless those involved appear on television on a newsmagazine show or a talk show to talk about their experiences. Similarly, no moral lessons can be truly learned unless it is revealed & pontificated upon on any number of national television call-in shows.

Freedom of speech guarantees that everyone must have their say; everyone must talk & speak & voice their every opinion & thought; from newspapers, magazines, radio shows, talk shows, call-in shows, soapboxes, electronic mail, the internet, skywriting, & graffiti, there is no shortage of quiet space that cannot be filled with the talk & chatter of American twang.

Lawsuits are the new form of activism. To make a difference in the community, you must sue your way across the political stratosphere, spinning courts & jury trials & giant cash settlements & punitive damages.

The supreme American ideal & its most prized commodity is Truth. It must be taught in school, invoked in discourse, preached from pulpits, stenciled on nuclear missiles & used in all its godlike glory.

A survey conducted among American homes found that 87 percent of the nation believes that Red, White & Blue are the primary colors of both pigment & light.

6.

In the night of ten million stars,
each so distinct in their own space
in the heavens, along a long straight
road that passes from one desert town
into another; Palm Desert, Indio,
Indian Hills, La Quinta; strip
mall upon strip mall, filled
with the Lego blocks of Americana;
the gods of the American Dream
buy and sell, offer discounts,
markdowns, special leasing deals
just for us. Each, none more carnivorous
than the next; resorts and hotels more opulent,
more elaborate, and totally disconnected
with the environment than the next:
Egyptian culture, Rome in the desert.
On a long straight road, driving
at night, the street lamps dimmed or spread
so far apart that the patches of darkness
in between seem something like comfort;
the blanket that covers us when we sleep
so trusting and secure in our own beds
in a world we will never truly own.

7.

My memories are stained with the familiar.

They are not perfumed with silence.

The round-trip ticket is inscribed in my punch-wild mind.

No luggage to check.

I have wanted too much for too long.

Not a smudge of this dust belongs to you.

Nothing true promised.

I cry for your vanity.

I search for your tender.

I wake for your savage affections.

I itch for an impenetrable contract.

Body permutates into falsehood.

Every queer chip clearly in place.

I have known too little for too long.

Queer for home.

Splendid refuge.

Return.

8.
I imagine America.

I see a sea of coffins, smooth & polished, twisted of fragrant wood,
      filled with potpourri & the ashes of Bibles.
& in these coffins, a sea of waxy bodies overpoweringly quiet, as in life
      & in death, fighting none, defying none;
carrion for crows & vultures to pluck & feed, for countless virus
      & bacteria to regenerate.
It is said that those who die too early, too soon before their time,

will come back as the most powerful ghosts, presiding over their
houses, dominant to a crushing fault;
but for those who die on schedule, there is no such power but what the
living do for them. In this ever imagined America, there lies a
haunting battle of such love; a distillation of a thousand century
beauty.
And here is the body that bears the contract of false colors, the scrutiny
of day & of night, of milk & of salt.
Here is the body that aims for the highest familial constellation, the
lowest degree of tractability.
Confronted by the great mirror of this love, I come deep & dark &
queer.
Confronted by the great mirror of America, I come queenly & elegiac, I
come intractable & longing;
burden of grief & hardship, burden of irretrievable tonnage, the
fluctuating stuff of hearts & lives, I come perpetually reconciled;
bellyful; pissing in my wake an antidote to bitterness.
Subjectifying my returning want & flesh from non-creation; returning a
crest of invisible skin; this is how I breathe in the pages of space &
pictures & peculiarity;
I will not make a silent sound; I will not be numbed by the misfortunes
of the present.
These are the last days here; & every approach now free from suspicion,
brimful of every silent right, falls into place; desire, mine; breath.
This is my occurrence. This is the sound of my indisputable body.
The necessity of speaking; the antidote to every bitterness, to all that
ails, to imagining America in our waking dreams & in our childlike
slumber; to imagining America in what remains,
& that which is hidden, that which hides, that which is blind, that which
sees all, which is unseen, which is unspeakable, unmentionable,
which dares not speak, which is whispered, which is true, which is
lies, which is punished, which is taken away,
& that which is time, that which is laughed at, that which is mistaken,
that which is illness, that which is granted, which must be repaid,
which is free, which is freedom, which is years, which challenges,
which is challenged, which ends all, which births, which passes,
which angers, is shame,
is no more.

9.

All you refugee dreamers & crocodile wrestlers,
I'm fumbling to make you American.

Everything has been swept away.

I see a history called lifetime.
I see a lifetime burning down.
I see the death of the body.
I see the death of the nation.
I see the death of the family.
I see the death of memory.
I see the death of nostalgia
I see the death of borders.
I see the death of the sky.

I create my culture everyday.
I write a bible of diaspora.
I piss in the embrace of men.
I bruise the broken speech.
I lullaby the dead in fields of fever.

And what are you going to do?
And what will you do?

I say I will find a new place that is mine.
I say I will find some place,

I say, I say, I say.

I'm imagining America.
I'm fumbling to make this mine.

The Real World

There is a real world.
It exists somewhere, outside

The focal point of my eyes,
Outside the timbre of my voice,
Way outside my pissing distance.

What is this real world?
It can be invaded

By aliens. It can close its borders.
I will find myself on the side
Of a barbed wire, thick as fingers,

Fence higher than God,
In the middle of a field

The size of a continent.
I will not know

Which side I am on,
No bearings, no markers,

Just endless field. A few trees.
Two small mammals. One marsupial.

My body spinning drunk. Pegged
In the sanctity of my deep dark blood.

Go there. Venture

To this real world.
Tell me how real it is.
Be my explorer.

Drink its murky uncharted water.
Tell me what it tastes like.

Tell me if parasites and amoebas

In its deceptively cool gulp

Will kill me, in this,
Our achingly craved real world.

The Men's Restroom at the INS Building

Cold marble, remnants from the building's past
when its sturdy quake-proof foundations
remembered what it was like to have
the country as its invading founders intended;
now, handed down from one governmental
budget to another, it harbors
what the country wants to be.

The thick insulated walls and double doors
of the restroom on the second floor of
the Immigration and Naturalization Services building
effectively muffle the sounds outside
its portals, so that the occupants can do
what all humans must do at some point, even here.

Every time the door cranks open
on its creaky rusted hinges,
the outside filters in. Immigrants:
tired, poor, hungry, huddled;
energetic, well-off, well-fed, unhuddled;
All, submissive as cattle, humbly waiting
for the butcher, passively queued in neat lines,
waiting for forms to fill, waiting to pay
another bloated fee; checkbooks, cash, money orders
in hand, paying for the privilege to file
document after document, and endless streams
of paper, in duplicates and copies and certified copies,
to be processed, stamped, approved, temporarily
approved, an identity issued, a documentation
procured, a proof in hand.
Until the expiration date creeps around
too soon, and the cycle begins anew.

The marble walls of the toilet stall
are covered with graffiti, Sharpie black,
written in firm brazen hand.
> *Tony was here.*
> *el norte.*
> *Roberto loves Suzie.*

PIGS! DEATH TO THE PIGS!
INS officers are assholes...
Who the fuck are you to tell me I can't stay in the country
This is the only place in this cold
building where anyone in those endless
lines can regain a sense of significance,
to hold heads up. But this self-worth
is short-lived when the door creaks open,
and the militant bellow of the country
protecting its land from sea to shining sea
percolates in: the rumble
of language difficulties, bilingualism
defeated and failed, fear
and incomprehension taking over.

Here, in the restroom on the second floor
of the Immigration and Naturalization Services building
the air can be very still, but each time
the door opens, the roil of deferred hope
and amputated convictions is enough
to quake the foundations to bombed rubble.

Smell

My grandmother loads the washing machine.
    I overhear her ask
                my mother why my clothes
smell *so funny.*

    It is the smell of raw lamb's meat.

My brother's clothes had
              a similar smell
when he came back from England, she said.

It is the smell of the West.

Mistranslations

Lesson #1:

How much is that pineapple?
(My, my, what a delicious tropical fruit.)
Berapa harga nanas itu?

May I haggle?
(I want to save US$0.20.)
Bolehkah saya tawar?

Can I get it for less?
(I want to save US$0.20.)
Tak boleh kurang lagi?

That is expensive.
(At Safeway in Mill Valley, this would cost US$8.99 even with my coupons and my club card.)
Itu mahal.

What is the fixed price?
(Give me a discount, you horrible darkie.)
Berapa harga pastinya?

Have you ever seen cockfighting?
(I love your culture when it is in your own country.)
Pernahkan anda melihat laga ayam?

It is a cruel act.
(Kill. Kill. I must see blood on this vacation. I have 15 more shots on my Instamatic camera.)
Itu perbuatan yang kejam.

This egg is fried.
(I know what I'm eating.)
Teloh ini digoreng.

Brokenhearted.
(You filthy whore. I'm paying you. How dare you. I can buy and sell your worthless cunt. Why won't you marry me and love me?)
Pata hati.

Let's eat!
(I love the cuisine of this country. I hope they washed their hands before preparing this meal.)
Mari kita makan!

The servant washed Mr. Smith's clothes.
(Domestic labor is so cheap.)
Orang gagi itu mencucci pakaian Encik Smith.

All my mangoes have been stolen!
(I can make an 800 percent profit reselling these mangoes at my local organic health food co-op.)
Habis buah manggaku dicuri!

No Won-Tons for Whitey

The special's not for you,
The brown rice much too white,
The soy sauce much too salty,
The noodles way too cheap.

No won-tons for whitey,
No nookie for you,
No razzle for baby,
No yum-yums for me.

Eros in Boystown

Eros stalks Boystown looking for his love. His quiver filled with fresh cut arrows dipped in the poison of his semen. His pockets bulge with his fattest wallet, and his arms jangle with gold and silver and diamonds dipped in cyanide.

Eros is a fat fairy in cut-offs and brand-name t-shirt armed with twelve native phrases he's learned on the airplane between in-flight movies and beef meals, ready to dazzle with witless wonderment. He knows how to say *please* in twelve dialects, *thank you* in six, *mine* in twenty, *love* in fourteen, and *fuck me* in one.

Eros lands on tropical soil and kisses it as if it were pilgrim earth. He breathes in the swirling dust and pollution, and in the cancered tissue of his ashen collapsing lungs, changes them to linen-fresh bacterial-cleansing deodorant bathwash, ready to kiss, ready for absolute hunger.

Eros is a 70-year-old Belgian whose collagen injections in his face are melting in the tropical heat, and oozing out of his pores, but he's got his young love stuck to his arm, ready to blot and wipe his liquefying youth off with a pack of disposable tissues.

Eros is a master archer, aiming his arrows with amazing precision, in spite of his Coke bottle glasses. Once he sets his sights on his target, and lays his bait of American dollars and promises of everlasting love wrapped up in the metallic giftwrap of migration to United States of Heaven, the poor love is blinded, hypnotized, lost, caught in the snare, doomed; that's when Eros shoots his carefully prepared arrow to pierce the heart and ass and eyes and scrotum.

Eros loves this land. He created it out of darkness. Pissed his seed into the land, dumped his napalm shit into it, fertilized it with mere pennies that he has found on the ground beside porno stores, decorated it with his wettest dreams and his scripture-blessed visions of snowy rapture, a diorama played out with natives reenacting his favorite movies with sticks and masks and dyed cotton loin cloths.

Eros bribes the psychoanalyst to justify his bliss, blesses the pornographer for helping him create utopia, attacks the poet for chronicling his destruction, and kisses the go-go dancer for his devotion.

Eros stalks Boystown, eyes half shut, flapping his tattered wings with the faded glory of a silent film star, cooing like a fiery infant, slinging his virulent arrows and darts maniacally, raving in life and death, setting his brand of chaos in motion, cutting down all obstructions, turning and turning in his mire and muck, buying and selling and trading his center, all the while, Third Eye infected and encrusted with pus, slouching towards Shangri-La.

Homomonument

The truth about Matthew Shepard needs to be known. He lived a Satanic lifestyle. He got himself killed trolling for anonymous homosexual sex in a bar at midnight. Unless he repented in the final hours of his life, he is in hell. He will be in hell for all eternity, 'where their worm dieth not, and the fire is not quenched.' (Mark 9:44) For each day that passes, he has only eternity to look forward to. All the candlelight vigils, all the tributes, all the acts of Congress, all the rulings by the Supreme Court of the United States, will not shorten his sentence by so much as one day. And all the riches of the world will not buy him one drop of water to cool his tongue.

—www.godhatesfags.com

Whatever Matthew was looking for — sex, or simply an evening of fun with new friends — he didn't find it, because he got pistol-whipped and left for dead... But many crimes happen to gay people because we unwittingly make ourselves vulnerable to attack. We trustingly, willingly — sometimes even avidly — invite strangers into our cars, our homes, our bodies. How does this disregard for personal safety happen so easily with us?...A horse won't put his hoofs on an unsafe bridge. But a gay man can meet Jeffrey Dahmer at a bar, and recklessly go right home with him... Gamblers who push their luck with the dice can wind up losing everything — and so can the gay man who pushes his social luck. Men who cruise public parks argue that they have a right to do this... but they are asking for their right to meet the Angel of Death... I'm not anti-sex or anti-love at all. What I am is anti-murder, anti-assault, anti-robbery, anti-rape.

— Patricia Nell Warren, "Looking For Mr. Goodbar...Gay Style: A commentary on Matthew Shepard's death." October 24, 1998

---

1. ANIMAL

i.
In the absence of any disease,
this is how we rot beneath our skins.

This is the test we are put to.

May we not fail so miserably
we are fed,
        human sacrifice,

to tigers.

ii.
What animals know is instinct.
Drawn inexplicably toward light,
food, water, shelter, warmth, salt.

What humans know is the burn:

> Mercy. Need. Careless sweat. Possibility.
> Treasure. Recklessness. The swoon of lovers.
> Electricity. Burden. Ash. Face. Appetite.
> Mothering. Apology. Impetuous lust. Temporary insanity.
> The gamble. Blind faith. An equally blind trust.
> Velvet. The imperfect pageant.

What humans know is hardly enough
for hooves or glue;

but ample enough to fuel our hearts
and all its immeasurable imaginary
landscapes and homes.

----

2. SHEPHERD

i.
This we know:

the boy, mere child,
pistol-whipped, lashed to the fence post,
a scarecrow in the savage Wyoming night
left for daybreak of gray field to find;

but there are no crows to scare away
from this barren wasteland,
no grain for morning birds to steal;

the only beating of black wings
came the night before;

and the bloody scarecrow
is powerless, can't shoo
the circling buzzards

looking for carrion,
to pluck.

ii.
This we are told:

the boy's face, mere child,
so clotted with blood
from his crown of wounds
that he looked unhuman;
animal, the witness said;

save for the tracks of tears,
a boy's tears, that cut
a salt river across the estuary
of blood and wound
revealing the tender skin beneath.

iii.
This we witness:

Another news report of another
killing, and yet another, and more,
statistics built like ash-fall
on every fag fix; every hunch shouldered
against the Angel of Death,

but it is no angel
even though it had wings and a halo
and papers identifying it as such;

for angels do not succumb
to gravity; they do not wield
their holy swords dripping with queer
blood on narrow roads lined with crows

beating their black wings, flapping
their hateful sermons of submission.

iv.
This we are faced with:

     The weeping mornings of nightsweats.

     A haunted mirror contaminated by distrust.

     The skepticism of the most powerful sinners.

     A pasture of sheep left to ravenous wolves.

v.
This, too, we witness:

Desire: rejuvenated, remade;

fresh out of the fusillade, unscathed,
fortified by the inferno and the plague,
nourished in insurrection's blood;

pure, unchallenged, potent,
resolute, uncompromised,
whole.

A separate beauty.

----

3. GOD

In this hour of trial
there is no arbor for me.

I cast no shadows
on walls as I walk

in all the glory
of my rushed blood.
I am either a ghost,
or there is no light,
not enough light to cast
that shadow I so
seek. My pupils
dilated to comic book
proportions. My bones
strain and creak;
my nerves spit fire.

My need and my desires
are gluttonous
in time of famine.

On the last stretch of street
to home, I stumble
over my clubbed feet,
I look up, and on
the side of the church,
beside the sex club,
illuminated by fluorescent tubes,
the pronouncement,
GOD IS NOT DEAD.

I have walked by this sign for years,
and not paid much attention to it;
but today, in the muddy clash
of life's intangible helix,
I wake to it, I take hope
for it is there for the taking.

If He is indeed not dead,
as I believe, evidenced by
protection in all the dark
faggot roads I've traveled on,
climbed through, bleed over,
then there is no fear.

The trials will cease.

My shadow will be restored.
Shelter will come.
Morphine will flow.
Famine will cease.

———————————

4. WORM

"...be known..."
The Jack drives up slowly
any number of times, winds down
his window, touches himself, shows you
his wad, *see no touch*, not until you go
down boogie, go down Moses,
go down, go down.

"...at midnight."
The house is built of straw.
The house is in the middle of a fire hazard.
The weather is dry, the winds brisk.
The brush is kindle-ready.
The spark is carelessly triggered.
The roof is indeed on fire
and we shall let the motherfucker burn.

"...all eternity..."
I could go on but it would be useless.

"...where their worm dieth not, and the fire is not quenched."
If you were in my body
      if my blood flowed
in your veins

I would save a taste for you.

"...only eternity..."
The King: I've yet to meet him,

though everyone in their quickening
burst of piss and cum swears
he is The King, Holy Hosanna,
Hallelujah, and so on and so forth.

*"...all the riches of the world will not buy him one drop of water to cool his
tongue."*
When I meet The King,
I will ask for

a new kingdom.

---

5. MONUMENT

Day shortens and frost pierces
flesh through bone; my eyeballs freeze
unless I blink like a mad cow, my bones
run arthritic.
    I am brought to this square
over the bridge and beside
the endless connecting canals
by the guidebook: its intriguing entry,
no description, just a red star
on the map where

I now am; and one word:

    Homomonument

Where was it? I wandered in search
of this monument to homo. Not knowing
that I was standing on it
the moment I got off the tram.

Triangle: simple geometry.
Unassuming architecture,
as if it were there, occurring naturally,
always there, part of the old old town,

but this monument, as all
monuments, is created:

Three triangles set
at each corner of a larger triangle.
One raised to a platform, one laid
in marbled floor, one four steps down
into the canal where someone has laid a bouquet
of chrysanthemums wrapped in purple crepe
paper, yellow clusters slightly
withered but the blooms still sustaining
their form and beauty in the cold air.

How perfect. How ordered.

Equilateral triangles within each other,
all obeying the laws of geometry,
the rules of which I learned
in primary school under the guidance
of compasses, protractors, and the math
teacher's stern ruler.
        Little did I know
the uses of this knowledge and its applications
in the world beyond chalk dust and homework.

A geometry so precise
it rules the natural world;
where everything creates
from precise proportions, precise
angles; even from the chaos
of persecution, the unbearables,
the shameful weight of history
seeded in this foundation,
                        it prevails;
the past, present and future, all time;
geometry, order;
                forms create within
forms, fold in and expand, sheer out,
repeat, obeying its own rhythm,
creating each and every
other endlessly, as time, as blood,

as heartbeat, as human bond is.

The plaque nearby reads:
This monument commemorates all women and men ever oppressed and persecuted because of their homosexuality; Supports the international lesbian and gay movement in their struggle against contempt, discrimination and oppression; Demonstrates we are not alone; Calls for persistent vigilance.

I wandered in search
of this monument to homo.
Not knowing I was

    its gravitational pull,
    its orbiting moon.

    its physics.

And I: $\dfrac{\text{struggle}}{\text{contempt}}$

And I: $\dfrac{\text{not}}{\text{alone}}$

And I: $\dfrac{\text{vigilant}}{\text{persistent}}$

And I wept.

---

6. ANGEL

There's a faggot on the streets
walking across the bleeding eternal
night, cruising for cold bone,
waiting for the vain spit
of night to turn, trading his butt
for shelter and more hollow promises,
trading good nights for less than good shit.

There's a queen running in the crack
and wail of alleyways and late-night crystal
binges, looking for smoky promises
in another run on the booty-bump,
and another palm full of rocks, and another,
until there is nothing but bone, cold
bone, drying in the unmerciful light of day.

In the downbeat of a life
hardly calculated
for the best piss of the pie,
I've been the faggot and the queen;

I've been nothing; and I've been
the fire the devil dies in.

There's a man inside of me
making his way up
the brilliance of my spilled
blood, looting my glossless obsolete
wealth, feasting on my ever-fatigued
wings,   *Oh cannibal, eat!*
              Be filled of your hunger.

In the swirl of common fortunes
and ignoble kicks, I grew
tired of the imprint of dark
streets in my mind, grew sick
of the blah-de-blah of goodwill and gawkers.
I made it to the other bloody
end of a pissy trip
with a shitty attitude.
Some luggage still intact.
Nothing to be too proud of.

I've been the hero,
the monster, the slut,
the piece of shit, some other
permutation of myself.
And even if I were Queen of the Universe,
the Superhero of the page,

I would still be selling my soul
to someone in outer-space
who is tending a garden of asses,
every one infinitely more beautiful than mine
ever was or could ever be.

I have nothing to say
that can change a mind
or tear a ribcage.
No knowledge that will save
anyone but myself.
These are things I know,
and these are things I will never know.

That in the early split of my secret dulling
when nothing is as light as my unbearable heart,
and nothing is as heavy as my untamable guts,
it will be as if the whole world turned day-glo
and I was the hero or the queen for just one day;

and I will walk these never-ending streets barefoot.

Everyday, I walk
through the valley of the shadow of death,
but I fear no evil.

I travel light.

---

7. REPENTANCE

Accept;
and here, the kingdom of heaven is open to you.
Here is our communion body.
Eaten of uncultivated epithets.
Drunk of every hard blow.
Digest its wounded meanings.
Savor its blooded appetite.
Blow upon blow until the soft body hardens.
We harden, we toughen, we cave.
We break, we rebuild, we recreate.

In the smacking fist, the piercing bullet.
In the detonating bomb.
Lewd flesh, virtuous flesh, shatters and wails.
A lament of unfettered brutal bearing.
Slack planets teeter off their orbits.
The universe slows to a passive slouch.
Plunges into deathly silence.
Extinction at hand.

Repent, the prophets cry, repent.
How would the meek know their true nature?
O those false prophets.
With mouths of rotting spit.
Teeth filled with five lifetimes of cadavers.
This, their immaculate condemnation.
Their flamed God's denunciation.
The symbol of years to come.
Nothing more than nothing less.
The prophesy of our end.
Our degenerate savage deaths.

Nothing more and still.
We defend, we fortify, we resist.
We endure.

We wage a war of no ruin.

Here,
if you accept, is the reminder of our Blood.
Potent in any state.
As valued as the first and last communion.
Here is the chaste body.
Removed from the maw of the beast.

All you faggot snakehandlers.
All you brilliant deacons.
All you diseased punks and punters.
I repent before you.

Guardian angels rest in seed.

I repent of God and his Devil.
Of Remorse and Grief until there is none such.
I repent Sleep. Exhaustion.
My Left Nipple. My Skin. My Tongue.
My Flesh, and there is still more flesh.
My Traded Hope, there is still more.
This Collected Rage, still more.
My Blindness.
This Exile. This Border

This Venom I repent

In faith, the body brutes repentance.

And here, and here again;
God the split skin.
The piss poor son of famine.
The stillborn blister.
God the genital scourge.
The flaming sore.
Leaves.

---

8. WAKE

Some days I awaken
from deep sleep. But instead
of the kiss from the Prince
on his White Horse, it's just the flies
buzzing about in my room
because I've left the windows open.

And all I want is: X
to mark the spot, a map out
of the maze I've declined to enter,
more than a moment of clarity,
the reverse of this decline,
one less wound, pretty things
to look in the eye,

a monument to nothing but
our incarnadine nature, a lament
for the last song in heaven,
a plague of irradiated blood flowing
now and forever, a dream
of a body full of memory, guttered
and sloshed and commanding my full attention,

the coming of the time we dream of,
a crucifix of queer flesh;

And at the moment of realization,
what I suspect might be my soul
will awaken and surrender, astonished

at my returning joy.

IV.

Now I'm rosebush and speak in rosebush language
And I say
Rise rose rorosarose
Rise rose to the day

—Vincente Huidobro, *Altazor: Canto V*

Little Everest In Your Palm
(for Meena)

i. LIKE FLIES

I should not have jumped
into a river the color
of milk tea, certainly not
with that gash in my knee.
Two Israeli hikers had already died
from flesh-eating bacteria
in the hospital early that week.
Fresh wound, not deep
enough to warrant first aid,
but deep enough to trickle
dog tick-sized beads of blood,
radiating its odor, invisible
to mere human olfactory senses.

Every time I look, I find
two green-black flies,
so large you could see their
compound eyes reflecting
the sun, stuck in the clotting.

I hoped the river water would clean
the wound, flush the untold
multitudinous germs that live
on the legs and lips of flies
off, but the cold milky water;

I'm told it is the clay of the bed
or the run-off of chalk from mountains.

And the river flows on,
and eventually, and after all

its meanders and detours, dammings
and spout-offs, after all the bathing
children, rafting tourists, outhouse
seepage, after all the endless

baskets of laundry pounded clean
with a flat rock, after all the
goats, cows, buffalo, oxen, chicken,
ducks and boar that swim,
drink, cool off and wallow,

the river flows into the Ganges
where it becomes holy, sacred, blessed.

Deadheads and hippies yearn
to join the local faithful poor
to be cleansed in it,
have their ashes poured
into its dingy flow.
Missionaries defy tradition
and history and baptize
their newly converted in it.

Endlessly, the people flock
to gaiety, celebration, joyfulness,
hope, prayer, reverence, mourning,
hunger, fulfillment, swindling,
extortion, haggling, soap-boxing,
political campaigning, bargaining,
negotiating, gawking.

The river flows to the ocean,
like greenbottle flies to fresh blood.
So are we drawn to our inestimable
useless fates.

ii. MATING SEASON

Monkeys on the roof of a Hindu temple. Cows
in a lakeside pasture. Grasshoppers atop the
crackle of a stone retaining wall. Fireflies
in the glower of the wild rhododendron bush.
Sparrows in the eaves of the primary school.
A German couple in Room 231 at the Mt. Fuji
Hotel, serenaded by the Symphonic Queen CD.

iii. FEED

The butterfly glides with the poise
of an seasoned parachutist.

Its wings like antique Victorian lace
hand-dyed lime green by samfooed maidens.

How it lands and folds
its wings, napkin-like.

Then takes off
in a jitter.

A mad beetle, phosphorescent
even in the blazing afternoon sun,

smashes into this elegant flutter,
grabs it with his horrible claws

and eats it.
Picks it rib-clean.

Every hungry species.
Feeding. Eats.

iv. NOWHERE

1.
In a chalky dried-up river bed,
a crew of men in their Y-front underpants

(green, red, purple,
brown —once white?—)

shovel granite rocks
onto the back of a lorry.

Rocks sent to the surrounding villages,
left in piles by the roadside.

Housewives and their children
come to take these stones:

hold down tin slates on the roof
make fences to pen cattle and fowl,

stack into walls to demarcate property,
dump into muddy ponds where once were roads.

Trucks, cars and bicycles totter
on the soggy stoned bogged path.

A tourist wades barefoot in the mud
puddle, slippers in her hand.

v. NEAR

In the distance, fog horns.
In front of me, grasshopper.

In the distance, firecrackers.
In front of me, Coca-Cola.

vi. NIGHTFALL

Katmandu:
The end of a party. Tuk-tuks and taxis
beeping and honking through unflinching
crowds. A man with a high voice shouts
for his friend to come down. Professional
mourners. Rattling shutters of sundry shops
closing. A family of stray dogs defend their
turf. Drunk European tourists singing and
stumbling back to the cheapest lodgings.

Pokhara:
The shrill of monkeys gossiping
from tree to tree. Hornbills
fighting at 3 a.m. Crickets.

Sarankot:
The innkeeper yells at a vendor. A restless
child cries. Someone halfway down the mountain
is being chastised. A goat gives birth. Roosters
crowing at 4 a.m. (In another country, this would
foretell an impending death.) Four mountain guides
snoring. A transistor radio blaring top Hindi hits.
The low roil of the coming storm. A fine cold rain
hitting a hundred thousand tin roofs across the valley.

vii. FAR

Ten thousand flightless birds.
Five hundred and forty-six water buffalo.
Four lost beetles.

No mention of catfish.

viii. A MILLION BLACK WINGS

The clay road speckled with black flecks
the size of rice grains. The torn wings
of millions of flying ants. Nocturnal creatures
doing the business of their species by moon cycles.
Attracted to moonlight, but fooled by the lamp left on
a bicycle leaning against the tin shed,
its batteries worn down, the filaments burnt.

And the early monsoon rains,
how it comes earlier each year.

The delicate wings fall off
so easily. One would think their maker
could have designed them better.
                              Flightless
and crawling, drowning in puddles of rainwater.
          Trampled underfoot by schoolchildren,
bullock carts, dogs, wandering pilgrims,
people with places to be, and a lone
      drifting traveler.

A million black wings torn, on
　　the sopping red clay path,
that ripple and shimmer and rush
　　and quaver with every
passing footfall.

ix. NOWHERE STILL

An old village woman carries
a giant wicker basket of hay,

eight times the size of her body,
like piggy-backing a baby elephant,

balanced on the back of her shoulders.
Her handbag rests between

the dirt-crusted basket
and the back of her wrapped head.

She puts the basket down by the dung heap,
puts her handbag on the hay.

It is a Gucci knock-off.

x. TODESANGST

Flies shoot in and out
of the dead man's mouth, nostrils, ears
and one eye socket, shooting
into one orifice and out another,
a rollercoaster of flies
circling, swarming, in
and out and around.
So many that the buzzing sounds
fake, like a non-too-scary scene
from a Hollywood-made TV show,
Rigor mortis had set in
and the body, dark and shriveled,

curled fetal, lay
at the side of the car park,
The begging children, the hawkers
selling cheaper souvenirs and cold soft
drinks, the taxi drivers, all ignore
the body: they have the business
of the living to do: work, sell, buy, live.

We are parked right next to the body
and we too look away, hold our breaths,
try not to breathe in the rot
and the germs of the dead. Dead
from illness, disease, poverty:

the dim grit of life.

We pay the entrance donation fee
and start climbing the stone steps,
careful to avoid the small pots of ash
and flowers, the banana leaf plates of rice
and ash, left as offering and memorial.

Sadhus sit in someone else's tomb,
beckoning those they think might be
tourists, the superstitious, those needing
answers or luck. The real deal
or mad men plagued with mental illnesses
beyond any gods' comprehension,
they offer their unwashed sage advice
for mere pennies, for whatever
it is worth, or taken.

At the top of the climb, we sit on the bluff
overlooking the temples. The temple monkeys
scamper out of crevices in the roofs and rafters
and play on the awnings, swing
from one holy place to another, playing,
fighting, mating, staking territory.
Hairless babies cling to their mothers' hair.
A few monkeys swing down to the flat
area in front of the river, only to be shushed
away by the attendants there.

One funeral is beginning; one is ending.
The attendant stacks bunches
of hay and kindling on the dressed body.
The fire he lights will be tended
for three days, until all that is left
of the dead will be ash, even most
of the skeleton will turn to gray-black ash,
save the bigger heavier bones.
Not even fire can rid all traces
of what was once living.
The fire burns out, and when everything
becomes harmless warm dust, it is swept
into the giant monsoon drain, where
it is carried away to the river, the sea.
The pyre is sprayed with the water hose,
and is prepared for the next dead.
        Stray dogs skulk the canal
for scraps of bones to gnaw.
Another attendant stands in the sludge
and uses a push-broom to help sweep
the river along. The litter
and the low tide are not helping the dead
go to where they must go.

These were the horrible ways to die:
Attacked by killer bees or assorted insects.
Stung by scorpions or bit by snakes.
Motor accidents on the endless highways.
Drowning in riptides at monsoon.
Airplane crash. Ferry capsizes.
Macheted to bloody death in race riots.
Murdered by burglars while one slept soundly.
Incurable diseases that eat the body alive.
But in it all, there is an unspoken deal
that the living will take care
of the dead: sent off on its way, funeral,
casket, cremation, services, memorials,
wakes, headstones, scattering of ashes;

precise rituals meant for the living
to go on living.

Back at the car, the driver is waiting
to take us to the restaurant for lunch.
Someone has covered the dead body
with a piece of thin cloth
which buzzes and vibrates
and lifts ever so slightly
even as there is
no trace of a breeze today.

V.

We drink our fill and still we thirst for more
Asking, 'If there's no heaven, what is this hunger for?'

—Emmylou Harris, *The Pearl*

My Weakness

1.

I was an unblemished youth in Oahu,
running in the humid cling of tropical faggotry,
unburdened by duties of filial piety and infinite honor,
I was free in my sallow ruin.
Returning homeless and wandering,
lived in the 7-Eleven parking lot for two days
until the local Teamsters boss took me in,
offered me a warm bed and pizza dinners,
put me up for three days;

His beer belly always cold,
his ugly dick Pekinese.

Found a rented room in someone's
garage; with no light to read except
by the phosphorous glare of street lamps;
roaches lived in the fridge and shared
my coldcuts and warm Coke; Matisse stains
of piss and fuck-juice on the mattress;
the smell of fish urine;
the rains seeped in through the seams
of wall and floor and roof, drip like rice
grains falling on eardrums; everything
crumbling and rotting and reeking
of mildew and recklessness.

2.

Lover wrapped in me,
if I ever knew better
I'd enjoy it more.

Pissed with some pink pills
you popped into my drunk mouth,
I will vomit blood.

Yes, it is damn right,
this relationship, lover

who calls me crazy,

ugly and old.

3.
Dire ill-reputed streets, draped with jittery
whores, gangbangers, dopeheads, psychos,
and 57 varieties of vomit and piss,
where the good people shudder to go,
or park their cars, or take a bus through,
or look out of the windows of the bus
as it trundles through.

But at this hour, drizzled
with the crack of dead morning,
the street is silent, cold,
and unbelievably safe. A lone
jitney chuffs along, picking up
laborers, and packing them
into its overstuffed belly.

I emerge from my weakness, fortified.

4.
I dream of my weakness. I kiss
my weakness on its mouth, take
its acrid smoke into my lungs. I wake
holding my breath, waiting for the intake,
the surge of toxic air into my chest.
The bitter saturation of spongy lung
tissue, mucus-coated with bile.
But there is no smoke, just dry
ionized air: oxygen and carbon dioxide,
flattened with nitrogen and laced
with the toxins and carcinogens,
the mocking wisps of a city respiring.

5.
Mirrors do not lie, even
in the swirl of smoke.

"Good shit," she said before
overdosing into a heap
on the living room carpet.
Her friends, panicked, yet not
wanting to waste the good rocks,
shoot her up with Folgers Instant,
call 911 and clear out.
We've switched your regular crank with Folgers,
let's see if you can tell the difference!

Shaken, not stirred.
With a twist. On the rocks.

6.
Chemical:
    bruiser.
    hardened vein.

Discover:
    how courage is redundant.
    unchallenged the richness of blood.

7.
I waited to be saved
but no one came

except my weakness.

"But weaknesses can't save,"
said the rabbit to the cat.

"They fumble, they flummox,
they bugger, they bewilder,
they menace, and they mangle,

"but save! Oh no, they surely
do *not* do that."

And the cat sighed and purred
and licked itself clean,
then turned its tail in resignation,
curled up and slept for eighteen days.

While the rabbit carried on
his marathon, eyes focused on the finishing line,
he did not see the hunter hiding
behind the ficus, who grabbed the bunny
by his floppy ears, shot him at close range
and gutted him for stew.

8.
Lived happily ever after lived happily
ever after; no happily ever after lived
happily ever after for ever and ever;
happily after lived happily ever after.

9.
Beauty is there for the taking.
Some folk know how to harvest fruit,
they know the season to pluck.
These are the ones who can fall
out of a moving car and still
stand up to rapturous applause.

Others will never know
the harvest season, forever
fated to cull bitter fruit.
They want too much out of life, more
so than anyone can ask for or imagine.
The seeds of their fruit are rotted
inside the green unripened flesh.
No biotechnology can make it lush.
It will cure nothing, learn
nothing, be nothing.

10.
My weakness chants its mantra in my ear.
Do it, it says. *Do it.*
It's so easy, the formula is already inscribed
in flesh upon flesh, scratched
so deep, it is fever.

#1 tried to do it: pills to induce
sleep, the plastic bag over the head,
the wet towel to keep the temperature down
and help the breathing slow to nothing,
but he woke with headache and the bag torn;
the human body tends towards survival
and does all it can to stay mortal.

#2 tells me of alcoholic blackouts
and waking on the floor
with the plastic bag clutched
so tightly in his hand
that his knuckles ached for days.

#3 was found breathing shallow
with the bag over his head,
not tied tight enough,
and the horrible horrible air seeped in
through the half-hearted loose noose.

Punishment disguised as healing,
they locked him in the Psych Ward at General.
And the only thing worse
than the Psych Ward at General
is the gay Psych Ward at General
where the fluorescent lights are on 24 hours,
the deranged scream bloody murder with lisps,
and the only sharp thing
in that hermetically sealed tomb
is the Mexican attendant's tongue
as it lays dormant till the special nights
where it resurrects as Esmeralda
at the drag extravaganza at Esta Noche,
lipsynching to the megamix

of Celia Cruz and Gloria Estefan tunes,
twirling the Tarantella
in faded crinoline and cha-cha heels from Payless.

But I have no bone for courage.

I have guilt.
I have fear.

I have my weakness
whose ravenous hunger
must be fed.

11.
This is what hunger is:

Accelerating while asleep at the wheel,
driving towards light and speed and water
and blood and cum, like vegetation's
tropic responses to basic needs.
If it's got and if it isn't got
I reach the same magnificent destination:
the diarrhea, the nausea, the aching,
the collapsing brain and breath.

This is also what hunger is:

The Zen approach: suicide by hunger.
After all those failed attempts at reading flesh,
he lay in all the beauty he could muster,
and waited for hunger to take its course.
And speck by speck, particle by particle,
fractioning the body, it did:

this is what hunger will do
to the willing.

This is what my weakness is to me.

False God Killed

The god
　(false)
in the guise of a monkey

appears

leaps off the page
turns into　　　　mosquito
　　　　　　　　pig
　　　　　　　　mountain
　　　　　　　　cloud
　　　　　　　　telephone book

so mischievous

threatens the dominant
　doctrine

too much to bear
this monkey

　　　　best thing to do

　kill him off.

How to do it:
　　　smash head with baseball bat
　　　fuck eight new strains of virus into ass
　　　blast shotgun in gut
　　　spit killer-bacteria into hamburger lunch
　　　suffocate with carbon monoxide.

Monkey/False God:　　　dead
　　　　　　　　　　　gone.

What Found

Cleopatra's palatial mansions
sunken beneath the Mediterranean,
its paved walkways and marble

splendor coated with algae,
seaweeds and barnacle.
The lost city of Pompeii,

time stopped and preserved
in the ember of volcanic ash.
A small red frog, no bigger

than a quail's egg, in the deep Amazon,
whose skin is as deadly poisonous
as the small red octopus, no bigger

than a sparrow's egg, in tidepools
of the Great Barrier Reef.
A planet so large and so far away

in the galaxy that if its hostile alien
patriots were to fire a death ray
that travels at the speed of light,

we and everyone we know will
be long dead before it even
enters our solar system to do its harm.

Dog Day

A long drive
before the highways were built,
driving past kampungs, padi fields
palm oil and rubber plantations,
small towns. Four ferries, thick wood planks
hewn together with rough rope
thick as a child's arm, all
bolstered by rubber tires,
powered by chugging motors to carry cars
in fours and fives across the sleepy river,
the harsh undercurrent lying under sluggish cover,

then bridges were built, then one ferry remained:
long wait, prayers that no river accident, drowning
death of family trapped in car to be recounted
in *The Star* the next morning; eventually,
the final bridge is built but the drives are
still long.

Looking out the window
counting milestones, watching the number
decrease by one, by one every mile.
Sometimes I close my eyes so the numbers
decrease by greater leaps.
                              Other cars
and other families, motorbikes
carrying a whole family to market, school
and back, timber lorries, timber lorries,
palm oil tankers.

Dad stops for a drink break, use the toilet.
Something cool and fizzy or black coffee
feels good on a day like this
driving long before new highways
are built to lessen the drive time.

At an open-air coffee shop, miles away
from home, the milestone counters
stopped, mangy strays wander

the streets, sniff and slink
around noodle hawker stalls built
on bicycles or motorcycles,
begging for a scrap, anything
to fill out those shredded mangy bones.
     Piss done, drinks on table.
A sad-eyed mongrel creeps by,
a piece of stolen buttered toast
in its salivating mouth.
Government health control officers come,
sweating in green-gray uniforms
lure the dogs out to a brick wall, promises
of meat and bones, fence them in
with their rifles, guns cracking
in the still-dead humid dog day afternoon.
We finish our drinks, get into the car,
the leather seats stick to legs uncovered
by shorts, exposed arms,
the sun-scorched smell of discount leather, sweat,
carry on driving, heading for home
trying to make it before the sunset.

Casted

Channel-surfing one night,
I came upon a charismatic
minister casting
demons out from bodies
of sinners. A long line of worshippers
formed, each seeking healing.
Bad heart, sprained ankles, high blood
pressure, bad cholesterol, manic depression,
polio, leukemia, cancer, cataracts,
an endless, endless litany of suffering.
One man, slight, mustached, sad,
wanted to be cured of
the demons of his homosexuality.
Laying hands on the homo's oily coifed head,
begone, the minister shouted, begone.
The man jerked, fell into spasms.
The demons are leaving him, the minister
preached to the congregation.
Poor homo: limp wrists
slishing back and forth,
like how you flick your hands dry
in public restrooms run out of paper towels,
as if the demons were being flicked
out of his wrists,
collapsed free of his shame.
The bible tells us that demons
cast out will look for new bodies
to possess, or they repossess
with the strength seven-strong.
Who will this man's demons take to
in that hall filled with, and sitting
in front of TV screens
across the nation,
the multitudes
of tender faiths?

Real Monster Movie

Monster, smelling of sulfur mire,
rises out of a hundred storm drains' muck.
Evil beast, looking not unlike Godzilla.
With scaly webbed monster feet,
it heavy-foots its way across town, wreaking
havoc. Stomping on highrise buildings, hotels,
skyscrapers, bridges, steakhouses, TV and radio
stations, convenience stores, souvenir
t-shirt stands, paying careful
attention to squish all phony
Polynesian restaurants in sight. Busload
of Japanese tourists think this is part
of their package tour. They throw themselves
in front of the monster's path, holding
up their fingers in peace signs, taking
Nikon souvenir snapshots. Half the city
is destroyed before the monster is wiped
out by an unrelated tidal wave. Surface
area to volume ratio and fatty tissue
buoyancy notwithstanding,
the monster, in gurgling roar, drowns
in the contaminated flood
waters. All the animals interned at the SPCA
drowned too. The zoo animals
would have perished but they all
burned to death in the Second Coming of Christ
two weeks earlier. The only things
that survived flood and fire were toothpicks,
ice cream sticks, playing cards, straight-edged
metal razors, commemorative dinner
plates (but not the matching accent pieces),
two spanners at the bike shop,
the only tandoori oven in town,
and all things made of balsam wood.

The Night

The hanged man smells funny
tonight. Loosen my girdle.
Light a candle. Tie me up.
Whose palm greets me. The bench
is rough. Put the flame
near my crack. Some
one will be hung.
A noose made out of check
ed tablecloth. Witch's
hats. Sailor's caps. Tie
my hands with hard twine.
My red stock
ings have runs. Are
sagging. Someone blonde is
watching. The hanged man's
veins rip his
calves are
broken. Blue.
I am counting
toes. 12. More.
There are feet that I
cannot see. The moon
is a crescent. Mere
smudge. Dust
spits out a dog.
Hides under the bench
with his butt stick
ing out. There
is some red in this
room. Drip. Whose
feet are those on your
shoulders. Where did they
come from. The dog's rib
shines. Tobacco
burning. Breathe. Scraw
ny arms that can't be held down.
Another man. Big. Rough.
Would look away.

Sleepless

See what goes on at night: Animals with flashing eyes walk on stilts carrying broken beer bottles; trees grow ears and lips and vulvas and sneak into your bed, slide under your covers; cockroaches and slugs metamorphosize into fat-free low-cholesterol pound cakes.

People who can't sleep don't have eyelids, or can't close them like fish and birds. People who can't sleep are destined to die with their eyes open. They know this and they obsessively watch TV shows where the actors sleep and dream and wake; and at every commercial break, they use the full force of their palms, sweaty from being clenched so long and tight, to push their elastic eyelids down, but the lids just won't close; it's as if they were rusty, exposed to sea air for too long, defective.

In real life, people who die with their eyes open can watch their funeral, their cremation; they will witness their bodies burning and their unclosed eyes popping in the hellish heat of the crematorium oven like chestnuts on hot coals. If they opt for the old-fashioned, they will watch their bodies slowly rotting in varnished sandalwood coffins until the muscle and tissue holding their uncovered eyes are devoured by mites and ants, and their ever-bugged eyes fall with a dull clank into hollowed skulls like marbles hitting the bottom of an empty fishbowl.

People who can't sleep do not have nightmares of violence; no dreams of hoofed or horned animals or root vegetables scheming to slice open their fat blue veins with the kitchen knife the moment they fall asleep; they never sleep afraid that other people who can't sleep will hurt them when they sleep. And when they wake from sleeplessness, the new day drags like old paint over their ever more cruel and pitiful skin, as if their aching flesh were merely a sad dream, remembered with utmost clarity, from an innocent childhood.

Single

Room 8, the cornermost on the first floor,
window borders the hotel sign, white
fluorescent tubes encased in white plastic
box, white light saves, makes weeds grow,
saves from pimps; this morning, a man asked
for a short-term room at the front desk,
his companion, a black girl, suspiciously
aged to middle-age looked lost, had a thick
crusty hide of ringworm around her neck, three
fingers thick, elephant-rough, centipede-red,
but he didn't seem to mind;

in the flick of the 60-watt lamp, baby
roaches, the size of crab lice, scamper
across the floor to eat
the stale sweat out of my underpants.

What Happened

Like when a heroine forces herself
into the fairy tale; when the best

part of the story is obscured by
the contrived moral; when the secret

motivation of the cartoon animal
is downplayed in favor of the falling

anvil; when the narrative spins out
of control, turns into a thunderstorm,

and pounds all understanding
into a magnificent flood.

Milestone

When the universe was so much smaller,
the entire world could fit in the palm

of your hand. There, simply, the rest
of your life was just that,

& you enjoyed every
single minute of it.

Blissfully ignorant, unaware
of the ever-expanding darkness,

steadfast & approaching,
all consuming;

where time & rest
grapple for fortunes,

& minutes accelerate
to crash into a sea

of insignificant
floundering gravity.

Chinese Gastrointestinal Tract Turns 30

O vile twisted gut,
why have you betrayed me
like a lover that leaves in the night?

O vile twisted gut,
just but ten years ago I comforted you
with early a.m. Egg McMuffins
after all-night clubbing and boozing
and torrid unrequited love affairs
But now, we have lunch and discuss our acid reflux.

I tended you with sashimi.

I fed you the best cuts of pork and then some.
Even in the Malaysian Encephalitis Outbreak of 1999,
I did not deny you your pleasures.

Like an anal retentive horticulturist,
— o nay, a loving mother —
I made certain the 1/2-pound burgers
were always smothered
in grilled onions and gray mustard.

I let you gorge on the fajita combo platter at Chevy's.
I gratified your junkie cravings of Mission burritos.

Together we conquered Meat Mountain at Hahn's Hibachi.
Did that not mean anything to you,
O vile twisted gut?

Did I not let you feast
on chow fun and pizza for breakfast?
Did the years of sausages and hot dogs
not delight you?

For you, did I not search the frozen tundra
of supermarkets and corner stores
for the kinds of ice cream that did not bloat you
and gas you in your lactose-lack?

Such was your beauty and your power,
O vile twisted gut,
No roasted fowl nor hog was too great for you.

Like an only child, I spoiled you
with 63 different kinds of tiramisu to date.

Ethnic food was your kingdom I let you rule over.

With my hand on the leash, you stalked
Vegas buffets like a cheetah on the veldts
where for you, I carefully plucked
the veggies out of dishes, waved away
filling salads, and empty carbohydrates aside
in favor of the chunks of meat and seafood.

I was your protector. I have not
subjected you to the whims and trends of the ages:
No colonics or pectates or wheatgrass juice.
Verily, was I not tempted
by the sign at the wheatgrass shack,
which promised "a fantastic release
of worms and mucous"? And yet again,
I deferred to your supple gastric charms.

Yes, once in a while I have had to run
roughage through you. But it was with love
that I did it, not disregard, and surely
you cannot hold such against me, my best intentions.

Were you not nursed
by Christmas dinners and Chinese New Year's feasts
and wedding banquets and well-catered social events?

But now, O vile twisted gut,
now, you are like a left lover
whose fingerprints
are all over my kitchenette.
Tonight, I will eat a whole fried Portuguese sausage,
and I will watch you writhe and twist
like the last dinosaur on earth,

not comforted that your suffering is mine
and ever more shall be.

Giant Non-Poisonous Snake

It was neither its venom,

       for what could any of us know
      . of its spit, its potency
       or deadliness, that it would hurt,
       sting, swell, but never kill humans,

nor its intent to attack,

       for it was content to sit
       in the dry drain warmed
       by the noon sun with its catch,
       a plump toad slow enough, unwitting
       enough, to be in the crab grass,

but its species, its ilk.
It was definitely its fangs,
and definitely its color,

       jet black scales worthy
       of an expensive evening handbag,

It was its slither and it was
that forked tongue that we could not see,
tucked underneath that petrified, slowly
digesting toad.

It was its reputation.

       Genesis. The Temptation.
       The forms the devil takes.
  "don't leave the cat's milk out overnight,
   it will attract cobras and other black snakes"

It had to be killed.

Two kettles are put on the stove:
Boiling water kills and disinfects.
   The first kettle's scald
would hurt, disorientate, weaken;
the second, if needed, if it could be poured,
since the snake would now be angrily lashing,
would weaken even more.
   Then the unrelenting blows from the bamboo canes
until the cord of black muscle lay lifeless.

The giant meat cleaver separates
the head from the body
in one hefty whack, an essential act,
                     who knows what sort of evil
                     will reanimate this dark thing,
                     this pawn of the devil.

The hewed head, jaws stretched
in ugly death, and its slack strained
body are picked up on the end of a cane
and tossed ten feet apart, back
into its grassy swamp home,
a warning to other snakes,
    poisonous or not.

The canes, defiled beyond saving, are wrapped
in layers of newspapers and thrown into the dustbin.
New canes will be bought from the market tomorrow.
The meat cleaver is soaked in boiling water for hours
to purge any hint of that evil blood.

And the spot of scalding and cleaving, stained
with spatter of thick dark blood blending into
the now powerless water, is doused
with bleach, and even more boiling water
and scrubbed, until
all traces of the clash,
                the actual fear, of such protection,
evaporates, and the garden
and the home and its inhabitants
are restored to safety.

Deck

The deck of cards,
the end result of a coupling:
King and Queen producing Child
    and numbers One through Ten.
Sometimes the Child is called
the Knave, the cheater, the fraud,
    not to be confused with
        the Joker,
who, in some games, is discarded;
and in others, the substitute for anything.

#1: sometimes called the Ace,
in some versions, the most powerful,
    the Alpha,
superseding all, its clean sharp
        isolated
pictogram lonely on the white surface;
in others it's simply singular,
    the smallest number,
        easily overcome.
#2: the ideal number, binary code,
    the theory of normalcy,
balance and equilibrium;
    we are not there yet.
Three: A crowd, but oh, so much fun,
    until competition sets in.
Four: Square, divisible, weak,
    perfect for boardgames, bridge, tennis.
Five: days till it is done.
Six: sounds like Luck in Cantonese.
Seven: holy holy holy.
Eight: arms to hold you.
Nine: days to go, close but no banana.
Ten: Oh baby of metric, meter and motion.

Dealt:
Fucked up beyond repair,
    everything ends
as everything is

supposed to end.
Some stupid Freudian thing
about that endless cycle of fuck-ups
piled one on top of the other,
a deck of cards,
          stacked to look
like a house, this little
pig made his house of straw,
one puff,
          pull the king
to get the ace and the whole
    thing crumbles.

In one version, the pig runs off
to the house of wood; in another,
it gets eaten.
          Wee wee wee
all the way home.
          The house
of bricks has yet to be built.

Puppy

The best part of a man and a dog
Is the muzzle then the paw.

In the muzzle, find mercy.
In the paw, find comfort.

The best dog in my life ended sadly:
Bowzer was put down
When his muzzle got too gray,
His legs too arthritic,
And his mind too muddled:
He wouldn't notice cars
Backing out of driveways anymore;
Our favors fell to the cat.

In cartoons, the feline and the canine
Are archetypal enemies, foils for comic plots;

Between your dog and my cat,
We find things to believe in,
Things to cross that divide of genetics
And evolution, evidence.

How you touch my cat with your rough fingers and
Take her to drink out of the faucet.
How your dog panics and howls
Like a cow at the abattoir
When you go running at the park
Leaving him with me,
His head on my lap,
We commiserate in our panic as
You slip out of our sight.

Mercy is falling asleep
In front of the telly
On a humid suburban California night
With the dog at our feet
The fleas biting,
Your mouth on my neck.

Is sleeping on my hard futon,
Our bodies twisted into shapes
That would disgust a chiropractor
So the cat can curl at blanket's edge.

This is what our animals tell me:

My passion for you is puppy strong
A gardenia floating in a dog's bowl.

Deal

Start with the dinosaur-shaped chicken nuggets,
the awfully cheap kind, mostly skin, feet
and tendons pulverized into a gristly chuck
that can only be good deep-fried in lard and eaten
in a diner laced with white bathroom tiles,
metal canteen tables and little children showing
their parents how animals copulate, all served
under the gaze of the big brown dog with a chef's hat dusty
from inviting the hungry, a stone's throw away
from the beach that lies across the highway (sea air's supposed to be
good for the soul), a much better class
of customer lies a spit away at the zoo.

Sad animals living in the wrong climate under
the watchful eyes of the paying public
who demand a show of all shows for their
bucks: eat something, scratch your pits,
play with those rubber toys, growl.
Watch the penguins stand with their wing-arms out,
relief from the heat in their Moses-themed pool
lined with reeds. The red-assed monkey clinging
to the wire cage pulling his butt hairs out.
The polar bear with fleas and skin allergies
gnawing on his arm. The Kodiak bear
about to die of heat stroke in his pen, which looks
not unlike the parking lot of a convenience store in Juneau.

Timing is everything. One false step to the salt-lick,
could have slept for three more hours
before going to the watering hole, and these animals
would still be free, not snagged and snared, hooked
and cargoed to this somber place. Timing could have sent them
to a better zoo, the ones where tropical rainforests
are created next to the savanna plains, so fur
and feather will remain gleaming, shiny,
groomed for all with admission tickets to see.

Other false move, and tiger's penis is served
in a bamboo steamer, bones brewed for aphrodisiac,

strength elixir, brand-name medicine sold
under counters while World Wildlife Fund monitors
shop for chinky souvenirs. One false move:
and bear's paw is stewed; antelope's horn is sawed;
elephant's tusk is carved into temple altar, paws
into wastebaskets, ears into fans; deer is delicious;
beaver is stuffed and put on mantle; kangaroo is dog food;
monkey is coconut-gathering friend; tiger is in magic show
in Vegas; baboon is heart transplant experiment;
orangutan is star of prime-time television sitcom;
rhino's horn is pickled; snake is broiled;
emu and ostrich taste like pork; iguana tastes like chicken;
chicken is skin and tendons, breaded in the shape of
ferocious Tyrannosaurus Rex, extinct, and his brutish
companion Brachiosaurus, extinct.

Start with a deliberate step, false even if you must.
Time it right, and irises bloom at night. Bergamot or bee
balm become the same medicine. Pomelos peel like grapes.
Forgiveness comes easy. Impatience and indecisiveness
as unsure as wild dreams. Cruelty and greed crumble
into heavy fools. Need is filled, gas station easy.
Tread in the tough language of a day, months,
a lifetime building up; anniversaries stacked babel-high.
If there is nothing but mere words, nothing
but time, I will squeeze my maudlin captive cravings
into a thousand cages filled with the beasts
of a million worlds. *Will you ever eat my heart?* Step
into the last empty cage, saved for us alone —

like fated animals and dinosaurs,
we are no more.